THE MUSEUM OF EAST ASIAN ART

INAUGURAL EXHIBITION

VOLUME I
CHINESE CERAMICS

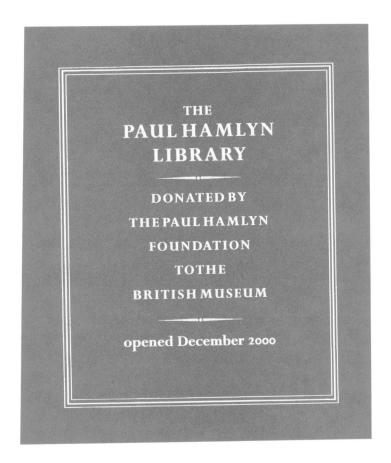

THE MUSEUM OF EAST ASIAN ART

INAUGURAL EXHIBITION

VOLUME 1~CHINESE CERAMICS

3 APRIL 1993
Circus Lodge 12 Bennett Street
Bath BA1 2QL England

THE MUSEUM OF EAST ASIAN ART

Published by The Museum of East Asian Art

ISBN 1 897734 00 X

Text by Brian Shane McElney, Honorary Curator
Chinese Translation by Ng Kai Yuen
Designed and produced by PPA Design Limited
Designers: Michelle Shek, Tracy Hoy
Photography by Arthur Kan
Colour Separations by Fung's Graphic Arts Co., Ltd.
Printed and bound in Hong Kong by
Hong Kong Prime Printing Co., Ltd.

PREFACE

It gives The Museum of East Asian Art the greatest pleasure to present this, the Inaugural Exhibition of its new museum devoted to East Asian art, at Circus Lodge, 12 Bennett Street, Bath, England. The Museum of East Asian Art was registered as a United Kingdom educational charity on the 27th of July 1990. Since registration it has pressed ahead with all speed to establish this, its new museum.

The two volume catalogue of this exhibition commemorates a significant event in the history of East Asian art in England. The opening of The Museum of East Asian Art provides the first new museum devoted entirely to the subject since the Gulbenkian Museum in Durham, now The Oriental Museum, opened its doors in 1960. It also adds greatly to the emphasis on the subject in the southwest of England, which already boasts the fine collection of Chinese art in the City Museum and Art Gallery, Bristol. This new museum will attract visitors from all over the world who can now visit both institutions in one visit to the southwest.

The concept and inspiration in bringing this project to fruition were of course those of Brian McElney, who, apart from the munificent gift of the major part of his private collection, has been the driving force in the acquisition of Circus Lodge and its conversion to a museum, and the employment of and cooperation with the distinguished architect, Michael Polkinghorne. Brian McElney, who has also undertaken the post of Honorary Curator for the next ten years, has also shared with us his insights on the pieces in the exhibition in the essays he has contributed to the exhibition catalogues.

The subjects chosen for the exhibition are Chinese ceramics, metalware and decorative arts other than jade, rhino horn and ivory. Jade has been excluded as this will shortly be the subject of a separate exhibition, and rhino horn and ivory have also been excluded because of the problems involved in exhibiting these items overseas as a result of the treaties on endangered species. It is hoped, however that a small exhibition devoted to rhino horn and ivory will be mounted by the museum at some time in the future.

The Chinese ceramics included in the Inaugural Exhibition cover a period from about 2500 B.C. to about 1820 A.D. and provide a fairly comprehensive display of many of the types produced in China during this long period, including many rare examples. The collection is particularly strong in examples from the Song period, which in the opinion of many experts is the most sophisticated period of Chinese art. The metalwares included in the exhibition range in date from at least 1600 B.C. to 1881 A.D. and include a number of pieces of great academic interest.

Acknowledgement must also be made to several other people, most notably to Robert Primrose and his wife Betty, who worked with Brian McElney in Hong Kong for many years. Robert strove prodigiously as Honorary Secretary from the inception of the project until the advent of Dawn Stollar, who has been the Administrator in the strenuous run-up to the opening and will, I am sure, be a tower of strength to Brian McElney in the future. Ann Sin should be thanked for her work in Hong Kong, Ng Kai Yuen for the Chinese translation of the essays and Elizabeth Carmo, now carrying out the secretarial work in Bath. The Hong Kong photographer Arthur Kan should also be congratulated on the colour photographs for the catalogues.

Finally, but not least, Brian Morgan, well known for his display skills, has given valuable advice.

R. B. Bluett
Chairman of the Board of The Museum of East Asian Art

BATH LOCATION MAP

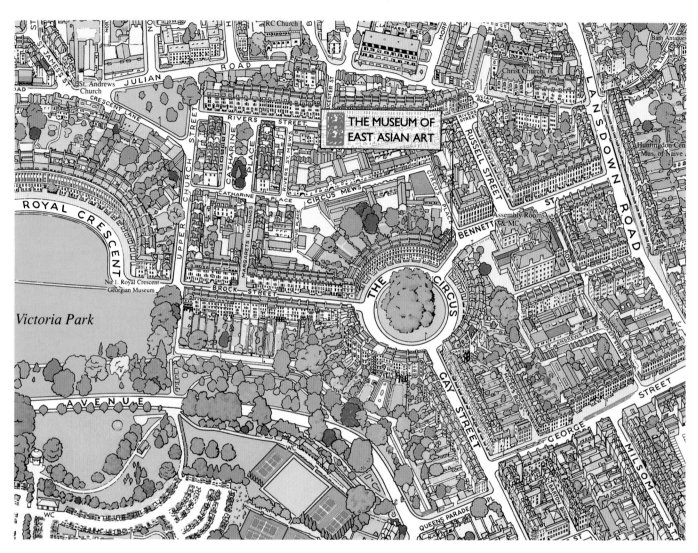

THE MUSEUM OF EAST ASIAN ART

AUTHOR'S NOTE

This volume of the catalogue for the Inaugural Exhibition of The Museum of East Asian Art contains the descriptions and photographs of some 225 Chinese ceramics, which cover the period from late Neolithic times (*circa* 2500 B.C.) to about 1820 A.D. and are a fairly comprehensive selection of the ceramics produced in China during this long period.

The author considers it unsatisfactory that in most museum catalogues in the past only a dynasty date has normally been assigned to a piece, where the piece is not marked by an imperial reign mark. This is particularly unsatisfactory where, as frequently happens, the dynasty assigned covers several centuries and a more accurate estimate of the age of the piece is possible. Whilst firm dating within a century is not really possible for many pieces prior to the Han dynasty, thereafter it seems to me that a curator should not avoid the issue and should assign the pieces in question to within the correct century of their production. This I have attempted to do in the textual descriptions included in the catalogue. On occasions, two centuries have been indicated (e.g. 12th to 13th century). I would assign a 68% probability that the piece was produced within the second half of the earlier century or the first half of the next century, and a 32% possibility of the piece being produced within the two centuries stated, outside the central period. As regards certain reigns such as that of Kangxi, which lasted for sixty years, I have in most instances divided them into early, middle and late periods.

Whilst most of the objects in the Inaugural Exhibition are owned by the museum, having been donated by the author, there are a small number of items that are only on long term loan. These items have been designated by an asterisk.

CHINESE CERAMICS

The ceramic art of China is one of the world's major art forms. High-fired ceramics were produced in China centuries before high-fired porcelains were produced elsewhere, and so famous were they that both the country and its ceramic products came to be called China. True porcelain, which requires firing at a temperature in excess of 1180°C, was traditionally thought to have been achieved in China in about the 10th century A.D., though in the decades since World War II, scientific evidence for firings at such a temperature dating back to as early as the Eastern Han dynasty has emerged. It seems probable that firing of ceramics at such a temperature even in the Shang dynasty will ultimately be verified. In the West, firing of high-fired porcelain does not seem to have occurred until about 1700.

Most of the ceramics which have survived from earlier periods were originally found in tombs where they have lain undisturbed for centuries. Ceramics were, however, extensively collected from at least the Song dynasty by the Chinese gentry. This coincided with the spreading to Japan of Zen Buddhism as well as the tea ceremony, which remains popular there to this day. This resulted in large collections of fine Chinese ceramics being formed in Japan where many now remain.

Ceramics, however, have been used from early times as utilitarian objects, such as cooking pots, cups, food dishes and water containers.

Production of ceramics in China appears to have commenced in the late 6th millenium B.C. in the central plains and the northwestern province of Gansu. Considerable pottery has been found in Neolithic tombs with some Neolithic cultures also having significant jade in their burials. The products concerned were pots, generally of red clay, made by building up rings of clay and smoothing the outer and inner surfaces to join the clay rings into the desired shape, which was then painted with black and sometimes also red pigments, generally in abstract or geometric designs. This type of pottery continued to be produced well into the 2nd millenium B.C. and over this long period, many regional types were produced. Several interesting and unusual Neolithic examples are included in this exhibition. The first example is an unusual double jar from the Machang stage of the Yangshao culture, 3rd millenium B.C. (Exhibit 1). It is interesting to speculate as to the purpose of this type of double jar. Perhaps it was used at the Neolithic equivalent of marriages. Next is a jar painted with a frieze of deer and a man with a bow and arrow in black on a red pigmented background. This jar (Exhibit 3), which I believe is unique, is from the Karuo culture of Qinghai Province in the northwest of China and dates to the late 3rd or early 2nd millenium B.C.. The other three pieces of Neolithic pottery included are (a) a rare Longshan black pottery beaker; this elegant and typically very thinly potted piece shows evidence of having been cast on a potter's wheel and was not built up in the usual manner of the red clay vessels (Exhibit 2). Similar examples datable to *circa* 2500 B.C. have been found in Shandong Province; (b) an example of the Xindian culture, late 2nd millenium B.C., with characteristic long handles and an unusual decoration of dancing figures (Exhibit 4) and (c) a three-legged container from the Qijia culture (Exhibit 5). The parallel of the shape of this latter vessel to bronze ritual vessels of the early Shang period is obvious and must be contemporary with that period in the 2nd millenium B.C..

The Shang dynasty tombs in China contained huge numbers of bronzes, jades, ceramics, horses, concubines, slaves and the like, when the occupant of the tomb was of a sufficiently high class. One has only to read the published reports of the enormous quantities of articles found in the tomb of Lady Fu Hao, one of the consorts of a king of the Shang dynasty, who died about 1400 B.C. to see the vast treasures with which the higher Chinese nobility were buried.

The burial of concubines and slaves to accompany their masters to the next world had virtually ceased before the end of the Warring States period with wood or ceramic figures substituting for them. Such human burials continued in outlying regions such as Nanyue well into the Han dynasty, as shown by the inclusion of slaves and concubines in the burial of the second king of Nanyue who died in 122 B.C. and whose tomb was found intact in Guangzhou a few years ago. Similarly, ceramic copies of objects originally made of bronze (Exhibits 7 and 9) or lacquer became common, and by the Han dynasty a large industry flourished with kiln sites all over China manufacturing ceramics specially for burial. Important tombs in the Han dynasty continued to contain bronze, lacquer and wood as well as ceramic objects, but ceramic horses and figures replaced the live horses and slaves buried with their masters in earlier periods.

The number of kilns operating in China in some early periods was enormous. One noted Chinese ceramic expert has suggested to me that during the Song dynasty there were at least 10,000 separate kilns in operation. Some of these kilns were large complexes and some were on a relatively small scale. The sheer number of centres of production means that it is frequently impossible, given the art historian's present state of knowledge, to ascertain that a piece was made at a particular kiln site unless there is something particularly distinctive about the body of the pieces produced at that kiln, such as the purple clay of Jian pieces (Exhibit 97) or the blue-grey body of some Cizhou wares (Exhibit 74). The best that can generally be done is to tentatively assign a northern or southern provenance to a piece but it is often impossible even to do this. It was not until the Yuan dynasty, when the centres of production became more concentrated and the products more specialised, that identification of the kiln site which produced the piece in question became much easier. I am told that the same phenomenon is evident with European ceramics such as Italian majolica and English Delft, namely that because of the numerous production centres it is often impossible to assign a place of production to a particular piece.

The dating of Chinese ceramics in the light of present knowledge is, as with European ceramics such as majolica and English Delft, normally much less of a problem, as shapes and decorative idioms that proved popular in one part of China were soon copied, as in Europe, by kilns in other areas. Technical improvements led to economies in production and therefore higher profits also spread like wild fire. Few art historians have emphasized how important the profit motive is in art history. I think its importance cannot be over emphasized. I have often been asked why I consider a piece to be genuine. This is generally an exercise based on knowledge and experience built up over many years. However, one factor that must obviously be taken into account is that the modern forger will not expend so much time and trouble on a piece if he ends up making a loss, so that the profit motive is also important for this reason.

It seems appropriate here to mention briefly examples of the technical improvements to which I have previously referred. Prior to the Tang dynasty, foot-rims were very rare, the bases of the earlier Tang and Six Dynasties pieces being normally solid (e.g. Exhibit 21). Such foot-rims as are found at this early stage are only evident on ceramic pieces that are direct copies of bronze originals where a solid foot, using too much expensive bronze and rendering the piece heavier than need be, would have been both economically and aesthetically undesirable. During the 9th century, the previous solid bases gave way to a *bi* foot with a shallow, wide, flat, normally unglazed base-ring. Exhibit 37 is an unusual example of such a *bi* foot, which is glazed and has minute spur marks. The 9th century also saw the introduction of a fairly broad square foot, on some of the finer white wares, and on pieces whose original shapes were probably of metallic inspiration (Exhibit 32). In the 10th century, well-formed narrow foot-rings came into almost universal use and the former broad *bi* foot-ring virtually disappeared. Indeed the only later wares on which I have seen such *bi* foot-rings are large jars of Henan *temmoku* such as Exhibit 75. This piece probably dates from the 11th century, and I think retention of the *bi* foot here is on account of the size of the piece. The new well-formed narrow foot-rings were technically an improvement on the earlier products as they used less clay. At first these new narrow foot-rims tended to splay outwards (e.g. Exhibit 47), but this feature seems to have disappeared in the early Northern Song.

Another technical innovation, which spread quickly, was the use of stepped saggars for firing bowls on unglazed rims. Probably first introduced at the Ding kilns in the second half of the 11th century, this method of firing enabled a tremendous increase in the number of pieces which could be fired at one time, thereby reducing dramatically the cost of production. I am told that the cost of fuel for firing used to amount to more than half the total cost of production. However, the use of stepped saggars resulted in unglazed mouth rims, which were frequently bound in metal (Exhibit 72).

One of the most interesting facts from a Chinese art historical viewpoint is the relatively abrupt change in ceramic shapes that seems to have occurred about the end of the Tang dynasty. The exuberance of the Tang seems to have given way to the studied sophistication of Song ceramics with virtually only the Liao dynasty, occupying that part of northern China which is roughly equivalent to Manchuria, continuing regularly to produce ceramics in shapes that can be directly traced back to the Tang dynasty, such as Exhibit 55. The reasons for this change are unclear but may well be connected with the increased popularity of the cult of tea, and the tendency encouraged by the cult to substitute cheaper ceramics for expensive metal and lacquer objects at this time. The cult of tea developed in Japan into the tea ceremony with its emphasis on ceramics of rustic charm. The development of the large export trade in ceramics in the Song dynasty may also have played its part in stimulating these changes. The changes in the shapes of bowls seem initially to have involved models taken from metal shapes (see Exhibits 44, 51 and 52), which in itself seems to confirm that one of the reasons for the change was intended substitution.

It is also, I think, worth noting in this connection that well into the Song period some ceramic kilns such as Cizhou and Xicun continued to imitate the ring-punched ground frequently found on silver from the Tang dynasty onwards, thereby confirming their decorative inspiration from metalware. Examples of this from the Cizhou kilns are Exhibits 50 and 61. As the Song dynasty progressed further changes took place to make the shapes of bowls conform better with the new techniques of the time, such as the stepped saggars already referred to.

Yet another technical innovation was the introduction of moulded decoration. By the Northern Song dynasty, moulds for shaping ceramic vessels already had a long history but it was not until the mid Northern Song that the use of moulds for the actual decoration became common. There are a number of Tang pieces which closely follow Sassanian or Chinese silver models on which moulded decoration is found, but they are rare and seldom successful. A successful example from the late Tang is Exhibit 38.

The decoration on Northern Song ceramics prior to about the mid 11th century usually took the form of carved or punched decoration (e.g. Exhibits 54 and 56). The problem with moulded decoration was the difficulty in getting a sufficiently clear moulded pattern when it was covered with glaze. This seems to have required extra care in refining the clay and ensuring that it was not damaged when lifted from the mould. The skills for consistent, good moulded decoration, I believe, seem to have first emerged during the Liao dynasty in the 11th century, possibly at one of the Ding kilns then under Liao domination. Exhibits 60 and 70 are fine examples of such early moulding. Exhibit 60 is probably a Liao example from such a Ding kiln and Exhibit 70 is almost identical to a sherd found in a Liao tomb dated 1057. My belief that the Liao potters were the first to regularly achieve good moulded decoration is reinforced by the interesting fact that good moulded decoration (sometimes even using Liao-type floral designs) seems to first occur on Korean celadons from about the second decade of the 12th century, during the troubled times just prior to the collapse of the Liao dynasty in 1125, probably as a result of an influx of Liao potters into Korea at the time.

Early moulded pieces were frequently tidied up by carving and occasionally both carved and moulded decoration are found on the same piece (e.g. Exhibit 86). By the Southern Song and Jin dynasties moulded decoration was common at many kilns, and was the preferred technique for the white glazed and *yingqing* pieces (Exhibits 88, 94 and 106). However, carved decoration continued to decorate many green wares (Exhibit 138) and the Jizhou kilns never seem to have used moulds for decoration, but provided ceramic diversity by the use of various alternative techniques such as painted or paper-cut decoration (Exhibits 105, 112 and 114).

In the Song dynasty the products of certain kilns seem to have so influenced the colour, shape and decoration of other production centres that whole groups of products can tentatively be assigned an approximate contemporaneous dating. These products are Ding, which influenced the ceramics of the 10th and 11th centuries, Ru which influenced 12th century ceramics and Jun which influenced 13th century products. Their respective influence even extended to other art forms such as jade, rhino horn carvings and bronze vessels, which are found in the shapes of Jun bowls or flower pots. Several examples of such influences in ceramics are included in the exhibition (e.g. Exhibits 105 and 110). More locally confined influences between different kilns are also found, such as those of the Ganzhou and Jizhou kilns situated near to each other in Jiangxi Province. The typical Ganzhou so-called rice-measure shape (Exhibit 127) (probably in fact a container for use in connection with the cult of tea) was copied by Jizhou and the glaze typical of Jizhou was copied by Ganzhou (Exhibit 120).

Many of the ceramics found in Han tombs are lead glazed, covered either with a green lead glaze, which turns silvery with degradation (Exhibit 14), or a brown lead glaze, which was less common. In addition to lead-glazed pieces, some pottery was unglazed (Exhibit 9) or was painted with red, black and/or white pigments (Exhibit 13). Occasionally blue, green, orange or yellow pigments were also added to the palette (Exhibit 10, 11 and 12). Lead glazed pottery seems to have been made for burial only. In the Eastern Han dynasty, the rich landlords of the time surrounded themselves in death with large numbers of ceramic figures, chariots, domestic servants, outhouses (Exhibit 17), duck ponds, pigstys, domestic animals and the like to simulate the daily round of life experienced by them on their large estates. I have even seen a model of a pigsty with a tired sow with suckling piglets and another in the process of being born.

Early glazed Chinese ceramics for general use, not necessarily intended for burial, can usefully be divided into three main categories: green wares, black wares and white wares.

The production of wares with a green iron oxide glaze fired at a high temperature can be dated back to the Shang dynasty, and by the 9th century B.C. such green wares were being produced in some quantity in both Anhui and Zhejiang Provinces. The wares at this time frequently had a basket-derived decoration. An example of this rare early type with an accidental bluish-white splash derived from wood ash accidentally falling on the piece during firing is included in the exhibition (Exhibit 6). Production of such wares, sometimes also with textile derived decor such as Exhibit 8, continued for many centuries. In the Eastern Han dynasty, these wares developed into early Yue wares with a glassy celadon green glaze. An example of Yue ware dating from the Eastern Han or shortly after, identical to sherds found at the Shangyu kiln site in Zhejiang, (Exhibit 16) is included in the exhibition. Further examples of Yue ware (Exhibits 18 and 19) are included in the exhibition dating from the 3rd or 4th century A.D. This type of ware was made in quite a number of places in China, principally in Zhejiang and Guangdong Provinces. The Guangdong wares, however, have fewer spur marks (seldom, if ever, more than five in number) than those of Zhejiang and never seem to have the brown spots, which occasionally occur on Zhejiang pieces such as Exhibits 18 and 19. One of the interesting things to note concerning these Yue wares is the move away from bronze and lacquer ware-derived shapes and the introduction of true and functional ceramic forms from Eastern Han onwards.

Green wares were the predominant non-funerary glazed wares produced during most of the period before the Tang dynasty and considerable strides were made in the production of such wares. The early Yue wares eventually developed into the classic Yue wares of the Five Dynasties and early Song periods (Exhibits 47 and 54), and ultimately into the classic celadon wares such as Exhibits 96 and 101.

The most famous of the green wares of the late Tang, Five Dynasties and early Northern Song period referred to in the old Chinese literature on ceramics was the so-called *mise* ware or 'secret colour' ware first made famous by the Wu kingdom in the late Five Dynasties and early Northern Song. *Mise* ware was known to be some form of celadon and was suspected to be a form of Yue ware, but this had never been archaeologically confirmed. One of the most interesting discoveries of recent years has been the several fine examples of celadon discovered in the foundations of the Famen temple at Fufeng, Shaanxi Province, where they were deposited between 868 and 874. These celadons were described in the written inventory buried in the temple's foundations as "mise ware" giving therefore a contemporary identification of *mise* ware. This confirmed the identification of *mise* ware with Yue ware of the finest quality and colour. Several Hong Kong collectors recently saw an exhibition in Beijing of the objects found at the Famen temple and they informed me that the green Jun saucer dish (Exhibit 64) is identical in glaze and colour to the excavated *mise* wares. However, the firing of Yue ware normally shows either a ring of silica chips or a ring of sand on the base (see Exhibits 47 and 54) and is quite different to the firing of the Jun saucer dish. In my opinion, Exhibit 64 is a very fine example of green Jun produced in the Northern Song period in imitation of *mise* ware. The saucer dish's shape and the squared unglazed foot are also typical Jun features and are quite different from the shape and foot found on Yue pieces. Green Jun normally has a more glassy, crackled glaze but this effect has been avoided here.

Similarly, in the early Southern Song Chinese potters tried deliberately to emulate the Korean celadons of the time. The Chinese writer Taiping Laoren in his Xiuzhongjin listed Korean celadons with other ceramic wares as "first under heaven" i.e. the finest of their class and, interestingly, referred to these celadons as "Korean mise" wares. The circular box (Exhibit 85) probably from the Longquan kiln is a good example of a Chinese celadon, copying a Korean celadon of the first half of the 12th century. The Korean celadons of the time, however, would have been fired on a ring of sand or on silica chips and these features do not occur on this Chinese piece. However, the design and colour accord well with the finest Korean products of the period *circa* 1120 - 1150. Interestingly enough, there were also included in this commentator's list the white wares of Ding, but surprisingly no other celadons of the time, such as Ru or Guan (nowadays considered the best categories of celadon in production at that time), were mentioned.

Celadons continued as one of the most important Chinese ceramic products throughout the Song, Yuan and Ming dynasties. A fairly comprehensive selection of green wares is included in the exhibition showing the changes in glazes and styles that took place over most of their long history. In the Song dynasty celadons were fired in a reducing atmosphere with a glaze containing 1-2% iron oxide. Also included in the exhibition in this category are examples of Guan as well as blue, green and splashed Jun and its imitators. Jun is normally classified among green wares as the glaze is also derived from iron oxide. The Guan pieces in the exhibition were all probably produced at Longquan. The products of this kiln and the Jiaotan kiln near Hangzhou are almost impossible to tell apart, the only difference being that the Longquan products seem to have a more compact body. Recent excavations of the Jiaotan kiln site were visited by the writer in November 1985. I was told by the official in charge of the excavation there that the excavations to date seem to indicate that all Guan-type pieces previously assigned to the Xiuneisi and Jiaotan kilns were the products of the Jiaotan kiln, thus bringing into serious question the very existence of a separate Xiuneisi kiln. However, literary sources seem to affirm the existence of the Xiuneisi kiln and alleged products of that kiln were included in an exhibition of Guan wares at the National Palace Museum, Taipei in early 1991, which I saw. I must confess, however, that I found the pieces so labelled indistinguishable from Guan pieces from the Jiaotan kiln.

I was also told during my visit to the Jiaotan kiln site in 1985 that the Guan wares from Jiaotan during the early Southern Song period had spur marks on the base similar to Ru wares, thus lending support to the tradition that the chief potters at Jiaotan came from the Ru kiln with the imperial court at the time of the fall of the Northern Song dynasty. One feature of many of these Guan wares is the thickness of the glaze in relation to the body, as demonstrated here by the small double gourd vase datable to the Yuan dynasty where the elephant heads on either side are so thickly covered with glaze as to be barely recognizable (Exhibit 132).

The next category of wares to be discussed is black wares. The glaze on these wares was also derived from an iron oxide glaze, but in this group the iron oxide content was increased to 7-10%. They were fired in a reduction firing where the amount of oxygen in the firing chambers of the kiln is reduced during the firing process to produce black wares and increased to produce red wares. Recent finds have established that wares glazed overall with black glaze seem to have been first produced in the Eastern Han dynasty at the Shangyu kilns in Zhejiang with a design similar to Exhibit 16. Black wares were initially made at the same kilns as the early green Yue wares, but later they became a speciality of certain kilns. An extremely early example of the deliberate use of black and brown glaze on bands in conjunction with an early Yue glaze, datable to the Eastern Han dynasty, is included as Exhibit 15. Soon afterwards in the Six Dynasties period, black wares became one of the specialities of the Deqing kilns, in Zhejiang Province. The most characteristic examples of the all-black wares produced at that time are the chicken-headed ewers, an example of which, probably from the Deqing kiln, is included in the exhibition (Exhibit 20). This piece is similar to an example recently excavated from a tomb dated 365 A.D.

Black wares, however, do not appear to have been all that popular until the late Tang dynasty, though in the 8th and 9th centuries, black wares, some splashed with phosphatic bluish-white splashes, were produced, often with features reminiscent of leather bottles, and are presently highly sought after (Exhibit 30). Probably as a result of the late Tang and Song poets and scholars praising the use of black bowls in connection with the drinking of tea, and the rise in popularity of Zen Buddhism, the quantities of black wares produced increased dramatically in the Song dynasty. They became one of the most popular types of wares to be produced during this period, with a large export production destined for Japan.

Their production seems to have occurred in many parts of China during the Song period, although the main centres of production were in Henan, Jiangxi, Fujian and Hebei Provinces.

The black wares exhibited include a rare black Ding pillow of typical light weight and fine-grained body (Exhibit 90), in contrast to the heavy coarse-grained body of the black Henan pillow (Exhibit 103), and an unusual black bowl of dark aubergine hue with rust decoration from the Yaozhou kiln, Shaanxi Province (Exhibit 93). There are also several black pieces from the Jizhou and Ganzhou kilns in Jiangxi Province, the Jian kiln in Fujian Province and the Cizhou, Henan and Shandong kilns, in particular, a Jizhou leaf bowl (Exhibit 98) as well as dated pieces from Jizhou, Cizhou and probably the Zibo kiln in Shandong (Exhibits 111, 143 and 91). In the later Song and Yuan dynasties the potters frequently made designs in rich metallic red-brown on the black background (Exhibits 125 and 126).

Rust-red glazed wares in the exhibition include, in particular, a red Ding bowl with cover, a red Yaozhou bowl and a red Dehua incense burner of the late Ming (Exhibits 99, 92 and 167). The Japanese have called the completely metallic brown or rust-red pieces 'persimmon *temmoku*', and one Japanese author has argued that they all come from Henan, but this is incorrect as rust-red Ding pieces found at the Ding kiln site in Yanshan are similar to that included in the exhibition (Exhibit 99). The Henan kilns and the Jian kilns in Fujian, however, also produced persimmon *temmoku*.

The bodies of the pieces from the kilns in Henan Province are a coarse buff colour (e.g. Exhibit 103), and those from the Jian kilns in Fujian are generally purplish or dark reddish-brown (e.g. Exhibit 97). The body of the rust-red Ding bowl is buff-white and almost transparent when held to the light. Even the Yaozhou kiln produced red and black wares of shapes and with a body typical of that kiln (Exhibits 92 and 93). The Cizhou black wares frequently have a distinctive blue-grey body (Exhibit 74).

Black wares seem to have gone out of fashion after the end of the Yuan dynasty, the only major group of kilns which continued their production being in Cizhou (Exhibit 143).

The other main group of early Chinese wares is white wares, in which category I include *yingqing* wares. It is this group that eventually developed into the fine high-fired porcelains that became so famous in the West. Fine white wares seem to have been first produced in the late Six Dynasties period during the 6th century. The subsequent development of the cult of tea and the use of fine porcelain for everyday use led to a great increase in the demand for white wares in the later part of the Tang dynasty. Exhibits 32 and 38 are white wares from the late Tang period. These wares were produced either at the Xing kilns or the Ding kilns, both in Hebei Province.

Undecorated white-glazed stoneware bowls with thickened rims and *bi*-type foot have been found in such quantities at the site of Samarra in Iraq that they are commonly called Samarra-type bowls. These Samarra-type bowls seem to have been produced by both the Xing and the Ding kilns and were extensively exported. Samarra was the site of an important centre in what is now Iraq, which flourished between about 838 and 883. The site was abandoned in 883 and not reoccupied, thus providing a valuable dating point for these bowls, though it is likely that their production continued into the first half of the 10th century. Indeed, I received probable confirmation of such continued production in early 1992 when I was shown in Manila several Samarra-type

bowls with a knife-parred slanting edge to their *bi* foot (this feature sufficing to identify them as Ding products; the similar Xing and Gongxian bowls both lack this feature). I also saw a Five Dynasties white bowl with a typical 10th century foot instead of the earlier *bi* foot. From my close examination of the glaze and body, I believe this latter piece also to be a product of the Ding kilns. The dealer related that these bowls had all come from a single tomb find on the island of Samar in the Philippines. The dealer stated he had been present when the tomb was emptied and he was therefore able to confirm their place of discovery and provenance. The Ding kilns initially produced plain undecorated white wares such as Samarra-type bowls. The Gongxian bowls are also distinguishable by having a sharply everted, rather than a thickened, rim. It was at the Gongxian kiln that Tang sherds of Samarra-type bowls decorated with underglaze blue were found.

The Northern Song court in the 10th century made the wares of the Ding kilns into an imperial product, which thereafter increased their popularity.

Whenever the products of one kiln, in this case Ding, became popular, the kilns had difficulty in satisfying the demand for their products and many other kilns in other parts of the country tried to emulate their success.

In the Northern Song, most of the Ding products were decorated with finely carved decoration. However, by the Jin dynasty fine moulded decoration replaced almost entirely such carved decoration. The Xing kilns themselves, which the Ding kiln had copied with the Samarra-type bowls in the late Tang dynasty, had become by the Jin dynasty imitators of Ding; Exhibit 88 may be such a piece. Exhibit 94 is a fine Jin dynasty classic moulded Ding piece, and Exhibits 95 and 124 are imitations from the Jiexiu and Huoxian kilns in Shanxi respectively.

The most famous of Ding's imitators however, were the kilns at Jingdezhen where production of white wares had already commenced before 1000 A.D. Initially the wares produced at these latter kilns tried to imitate the lovely yellowish-white colour of the Ding wares, but at some time during the second half of the 11th century, the Jingdezhen potters managed to deliberately achieve the marvelous sky-blue glaze (caused by slight iron oxide impurities either in the clay or glaze material) of *yingqing* at its finest. In the first half of the 11th century such sky-blue glaze was rare and probably accidental. Exhibits 58, 59 and 76 represent products of the Jingdezhen kilns, the first two from the first half of the 11th century and the third from about 1100. These *yingqing* wares were the progenitors of the *shufu* wares of the Yuan dynasty, the white wares of the Ming and Qing dynasties, and the blue and white and later wares of the Yuan, Ming and Qing dynasties. Jingdezhen ultimately became the predominant centre in China for the production of fine quality ceramics. White wares also became the speciality of the Dehua kilns in Fujian where the famous *blanc-de-chine* ware was produced.

Included in the exhibition is a range of white wares dating from between the 9th and the 18th centuries. Most of these were produced at Jingdezhen. However, in addition to the white wares from Ding and its imitators

already mentioned, examples from Dehua (Exhibits 165 and 166) and elsewhere (Exhibits 43, 45 and 48) are also included.

Falling outside the three main categories I have mentioned are the polychrome wares, either lead glazed or not. I am referring here to wares with more than one glaze colour and not unglazed pieces painted with various coloured pigments or monochrome pieces with gilding. Prior to the Tang dynasty, green wares were occasionally found with iron-brown spots (Exhibit 19) or patches of iron-brown, and such wares continued into the Tang dynasty. The most famous polychrome ceramic wares of this early period, however, were the Tang *sancai* pieces which were decorated with lead-based glazes of brown, green and yellowish-white colour (Exhibit 28). Production of these spectacular wares probably started in the second half of the 7th century, with the rare colour blue being added to the colour palette later. The approximate date for its inclusion in the palette is still uncertain. A piece with blue colour was found in a tomb dated 723, and a rather ambiguous report exists of a find in the tomb of Zheng Rentai dated 664. If this is correct, it is very surprising that not a single piece with blue decoration was found in the rich tomb of Princess Yongtai dated 706 or any other dated tomb between 664 and 723. These *sancai* pieces became very popular and were produced in considerable quantities for the nobility until the Aulushan rebellion in 756 or the Tibetan invasion of 763. Thereafter, their production dropped to almost nothing until it was revived during the Liao dynasty in the mid-11th century.

Examples of classic *sancai* ware, one with

blue glaze in wax-resist technique dating probably from the first half of the 8th century, are included in the exhibition (Exhibits 28 and 29) as well as a Cizhou pillow from the 12th century (Exhibit 87). Examples of polychrome Liao ware are Exhibits 71 and 100.

One of the most important things to note on the Tang lead glaze pieces is the importance of the white glaze or slip. If the white glaze or slip is good then the ceramic tends to come out extremely well (Exhibit 27), but if the white glaze is poor this does not occur.

One of the interesting techniques used by the Chinese potters is marbled ware. In this ware, clays of different colours are kneaded together, and when the clay has been dried out to a leathery hardness, the outside layer is shaved and the whole piece then covered with a transparent coloured glaze normally of either green, brown or yellow colour. The different coloured clays under the glaze give a marbled effect to the glazed piece. This type of ware was first introduced in China in the Tang dynasty and Tang brown and green glazed examples are included in the exhibition (Exhibits 25 and 26). Soon after the introduction of marbled ware, a variant was introduced whereby marbleized clay sections were inserted into an otherwise one-colour clay piece and then glazed over. This variant was especially popular in pottery pillows from the mid Tang onwards. The third marbling technique used was to build up the marbleized clay on an otherwise solid, one colour clay base or rim. This variant seems to have been introduced into the ceramic repertoire towards the end of the Tang dynasty and was the technique commonly used thereafter. Examples of this third technique

dating from the late Tang and Northern Song are included (Exhibits 36 and 72).

Marbled ware, however, involves quite considerable skill and a great deal of extra work in the careful shaving of the piece to avoid smudging of the clay colours. In the Northern Song, therefore, simulated marbled ware was produced whereby different coloured slips were painted onto the single coloured clay pot to simulate marbled ware. An example of this comparatively rare type is Exhibit 73. After the Northern Song period, marbled ware seems to have fallen out of favour and does not appear to have been produced thereafter other than as deliberate copies of earlier types.

The Jin dynasty produced the first polychrome glazed examples not based on lead-based glazes at the Cizhou kilns. Cizhou ceramics almost invariably have a white slip to cover the relatively coarse body material generally of grey or buff colour, which was then fired to a relatively high temperature. Overglaze polychrome colours are then applied in a second firing at a much lower temperature. These kilns used various iron oxide glazes over the white slip in this second firing to produce the coloured glazes desired. The overglaze enamels so produced were initially either green, yellow, *rouge-de-fer* (iron-red) or black in colour. The traditional date for the introduction of such overglaze coloured enamels is just prior to 1200. However I was surprised to see at the Cernuschi museum in Paris a sherd of a figure with such overglaze enamels marked as having come from Qinghexian or Juluxian, which were inundated by the Yangzi River in 1108 so that an earlier date for such introduction seems probable. A rare example of this technique is the polychrome figure dating from the 13th century exhibited here (Exhibit 123). The use of such overglaze enamels, once introduced, gained in popularity with other colours, such as aubergine, being progressively added to the palette. By the Qing dynasty such overglaze polychromes had almost entirely superseded the earlier polychroming techniques using lead based glazes. Another overglaze enamelled piece roughly contemporaneous to the Cizhou polychrome piece but from the Hengshan kiln, Hunan(Exhibit 109), and overglaze polychrome enamels from the Ming and Qing are included in this exhibition (e.g. Exhibits 150, 155, 158, 179, 183 and 184).

One of the interesting groups to appear in recent years is comprised of spotted white wares, the decoration consisting of a number of ferruginous brown spots under a white glaze. In the past twenty years, many pieces with brown-splashed decoration but under a *yingqing* bluish-white glaze or on a celadon piece have been found in Indonesia and the Philippines. These are much more familiar objects, and examples dating from the late Southern Song or Yuan dynasty are in the exhibition (Exhibits 134 and 139). In more recent years, however, numerous figures, animals and other objects with similar splashed decoration but under a yellowish, greenish-white or early *yingqing* glaze have come to light. The place of production of this interesting group is presently uncertain, but some similar objects were excavated from a grave near Jingdezhen in 1966 and I believe that grave has been dated to the first half of the 11th century. There is certainly at least one of this class of ware in the Jingdezhen Museum to which the curator assigned a Northern Song

date. He stated to me, however, that it was not made at Jingdezhen. This class of ware can be distinguished from the late Song to Yuan pieces with brown splashes under a *yingqing* or *shufu*-like glaze (Exhibit 139) by the yellowish-white glaze covering the brown spots. This glaze is clearly more related to the glaze found on white wares dating to the Five Dynasties and on early *yingqing* wares of the early Northern Song periods than to the bluish glaze of the late Song/Yuan *yingqing* and *shufu* wares. Four pieces of this interesting early group are included in the exhibition (Exhibits 65, 66, 67 and 68). A man-headed fish dated to the Five Dynasties period and similar to Exhibit 66 but unglazed is exhibited in the Nanjing Museum.

Another interesting piece with such spots is the rare phoenix-headed ewer (Exhibit 53), probably from the late Five Dynasties period. This ewer, with its well sculpted phoenix head, harks back to ewers of the Tang dynasty. It is similar to a famous piece in the collection of the British Museum, which has been dated to the Northern Song. The British Museum piece, however, has an additional decorative band of stamped flower heads, a feature used on many Guangdong pieces exported to the Philippines in the early Northern Song. The absence of this band possibly indicates production in the Five Dynasties period when production for export was not so prevalent. Both the British Museum example and Exhibit 53 are thought to be from the Chaozhou kiln in Guangdong Province.

Other interesting objects of the Tang, Five Dynasties and Song periods are a small covered Tang dynasty box with black decoration from the Yaozhou kiln, Shaanxi Province (Exhibit 34), and a group of pieces from Jiexiu (Exhibits 95, 116 and 117), and Hunyuan (Exhibits 42 and 104), both in Shanxi Province, and Nanfeng, Jiangxi Province, (Exhibit No.121), all similar to sherds which were included in the Kiln Sherds Exhibition held at the Ashmolean Museum, Oxford in 1980 and later at the Fung Pingshan Museum in Hong Kong. An interesting characteristic of some of the Jin dynasty bowls from the Shanxi kilns of Jiexiu and Hunyuan is the unglazed ring for stacking in the bowl's interior. The piece from the Hengshan kiln in Hunan Province (Exhibit 109) is similar to a sherd published in a recent Chinese publication.

Emphasis has been deliberately placed on the later ceramic pieces of unusual types as many other exhibitions have already illustrated the classic wares of the Ming and Qing dynasties. From the Ming dynasty, for instance, are an unusual polychrome biscuit piece (Exhibit 151), both an aubergine and a red *kinrande* (Exhibits 152 and 153), green-yellow and aubergine glazed sculptures of two immortals as incense stick holders on high-holed pedestals comparable to contemporary late Ming ivories (Exhibit 164), and a coffee-glazed piece with underglaze blue and black glaze (Exhibit 162).

From the Qing dynasty, there is a fine early Chinese imitation of Japanese Imari ware (Exhibit 186), a jardiniere imitating pudding stone (Exhibit 220), and two variants of robin's egg glaze (Exhibit 206 and 221).

Prior to approximately 1683, the blue used on polychrome pieces was almost always underglaze blue (Exhibits 155 and 174), but after that date overglaze blue came into common use and formed one of the most important colours of the *famille verte* palette. Some overglaze cobalt blue is found in the late Transitional period, but it is very rare. Only one earlier piece of overglaze cobalt blue is known, a Jiajing marked piece in the British Museum collection. It is thought to be of mid 16th century date but I have not seen it. The hexagonal stem cup is (Exhibit 184) is an early *famille verte* piece with both underglaze and overglaze blue. *Famille verte* wares, which typically use overglaze blue, involve the firing of all the overglaze enamels at once, at relatively low temperatures, thus minimizing the possibility of misfiring. The use of overglaze cobalt blue, however, first became common after 1680; the use of both underglaze and overglaze blue on Exhibit 184 suggests a date in the mid 1680s for this piece. A white glazed body with underglaze blue mark or outlines, as in the *doucai* pieces, would of course still have required an initial firing at over 1180°C. The Chinese vase imitating Japanese Imari ware (Exhibit 186), I believe can also be dated with confidence to the late 1690s. The kilns at Jingdezhen were closed from 1677 to 1683 by the Rebellion of the Three Feudatories. During this closure European buyers sourced their fine ceramics in Japan, and thus Kakiemon and Imari pieces were exported in large quantities to Europe at this time and became popular. The typical Imari palette, which was particularly rich in *rouge-de-fer* and underglaze blue, both enriched with gold, seems to have first been used in pieces supplied to European palaces in the early 1690s and became very popular at the time. Apart from the use of the classic Imari palette, Exhibit 186 has several typical Japanese features such as the circular mons with tassels. One of the panels even depicts a chrysanthemum and rock drawn very much in the Imari style. The sheer quality of this vase, arguably much superior to the Japanese Imari of the time was, I believe, a deliberate attempt to compete with Japanese Imari shortly after it had become popular.

The Qing dynasty produced enormous quantities of ceramics, many of which were of fine quality. Indeed, from a technical point of view the reign of Yongzheng (1723 - 1735) probably represents the high watermark of technical achievement in this field. Many commentators consider that no finer nor more technically perfect pieces than the imperial ceramic products of this period have been produced anywhere in the world. Several examples from this period have been included in this exhibition, such as Exhibit 196 which has underglaze red of the finest quality. This particular colour was very difficult to fire successfully and few examples are technically perfect, but by the Yongzheng period the defects had been completely ironed out. Almost perfect underglaze red coupled with underglaze blue was achieved in the early Kangxi period and an example dated to the year 1671 is included in the exhibition (Exhibit 175).

Arguably the best ceramic productions of the Qing dynasty are the monochrome wares. All the monochrome products of earlier periods continued to be produced in the Qing. These include imperial yellow (Exhibit 205), white wares (Exhibit 190), tea dust (Exhibit 213), Guan (Exhibit 212) and celadons (Exhibits 214 and 215). Fine blue and white pieces in Ming style (Exhibits 193, 194 and 195) were also among the best products of the period. New or improved monochromes were produced, such as mirror-black, peach-bloom (Exhibit 192), *clair-de-lune* (Exhibit 217), dark and pale aubergine (Exhibits 191 and 203), emerald-green (Exhibit 204) and Langyao (Exhibit 182). In November 1985, at the site of the Qing imperial kiln at Jingdezhen, I picked up a sherd of a saucer identical to Exhibit 203. All structures on the site had been destroyed during the Cultural Revolution, and nothing remained when I saw it but a weed-infested hill covered with sherds of high-quality ceramics.

The imperial factories at Jingdezhen from 1683 on were under strict imperial control, and many innovative pieces and colour schemes were produced, particularly after 1770 in the middle of Qianlong's reign, at which time the potters tried to imitate in ceramics other media such as pudding stone (Exhibit 220) and bronze. One of the interesting glazes produced in the mid Qing period is robin's egg glaze. This was first produced experimentally in the reign of Yongzheng and perfected in the Qianlong period. A marked Yongzheng example (Exhibit 206) and another with a green variant of robin's egg glaze with a Qianlong mark (Exhibit 221) are included in the exhibition. The glaze on the Yongzheng example shows the incomplete fusion of the glaze colours normally found during the Yongzheng period. The Qianlong example shows the complete fusion of glaze colours achieved by that reign.

Copies of wares from earlier periods were also made. These include the famous Chenghua *doucai* chicken cups (Exhibit 189), and those with European-type decoration and colours (Exhibits 207, 209 and 210). Indeed, the Jesuits at the Chinese imperial court are known to have given examples of Limoges enamels to the Qing enamellers for copying. Six extant examples are known to have been copied from Limoges enamels, no doubt derived from the prototypes supplied by the Jesuits. All six show the initials of the Limoges enameller Jacques Laudin (1627-1695) or his nephew of the same name (1663-1729) which no doubt also appeared on the originals. The actual designs on the Chinese ceramics were subtly changed from their Limoges prototypes. One of two known examples of the same shape is included in the exhibition (Exhibit 185), the other being in the Victoria and Albert Museum.

One of the more interesting groups of Qing ceramics included in the exhibition are those blue and white pieces (sometimes also with underglaze red) decorated with pencil drawing rather than washes, commonly called the 'Master of the Rocks' style (Exhibits 171 and 175). Until recently the dating of this group and other related pieces has been controversial. While Chinese experts insisted on dating the group to the late Kangxi/early Yongzheng (*circa* 1720), their European counterparts tended to date the group from about 1660 to 1675. Apart from the fine pencil drawings of mountains, the group is also frequently characterized by distinctive borders such as the so-called cracked-ice decoration, pine needles or groups of dots drawn with a wet brush. The dating of the Master of the Rocks group to the 1660-1675 period is now generally agreed. Exhibit 175 and similar pieces dated both by cyclical date and reign mark to 1671-1674 have assisted in settling this argument.

Another controversial group was the Transitional wares with 'v-tick' grasses (e.g.

Exhibit 168). These were sometimes inscribed with cyclical dates, which European commentators (noting the depiction of similar pieces in Dutch genre paintings of the 1660s) dated from 1636 to 1643. Here again the Chinese insisted on dating this group sixty years later. However, in the last year or so, the Chinese have published a blue and white censer with 'v-tick' grasses, which is dated with a cyclical date and Chongzhen reign mark to the 1640s, thus settling once and for all the dating of the 'v-tick' group. The earliest cyclically dated piece with 'v-tick' grasses I have seen was, so far as I can recall, 1625. I cannot recall having seen any of this group with cyclical dates later than 1650.

Increasingly from the beginning of the 18th century, Chinese ceramics were decorated to European order with armorial bearings. It is relatively easy to trace the family for which these armorial services were made. Before the 18th century, such armorial porcelains are relatively rare though they do exist from about the reign of Jiajing (1522-1566). Initially the armorials were confined to Portuguese families, the carriage of Chinese ceramics to Europe having been almost a Portuguese/Spanish monopoly until approximately 1600. Thereafter this monopoly was increasingly replaced by an effective Dutch monopoly which lasted until approximately the end of the 17th century, with most armorial designs relating to Dutch families. During the 18th century, the various European powers with factories in Canton all carried Chinese ceramics to Europe. Many of the armorial porcelain decorated in China during this century were supplied to the order of English families. Exhibit 215 is an example from such a dinner service supplied to an English family in the second quarter of the 18th century. Numerous such services were supplied to residents of Bath, and the great expert on Chinese armorial porcelains is presently a resident of this city. These armorial porcelains have become, in recent decades, an interesting study in themselves, combining as they do knowledge of Chinese ceramics with a knowledge of heraldry and genealogy. The production of such armorial porcelains continued until about 1850. There was, however, a considerable decline in quality during the 19th century.

It has frequently been suggested by experts that the ceramics of the 19th century were much inferior to those produced before 1800. This is a dangerous generalisation, though there is no doubt that there was a tendency after 1800 towards over-decoration. Although the 19th century was a period when China was historically in decline with considerable internal strife, fine ceramics nevertheless continued to be produced. Many of the best Yixing pieces were made during the first half of the 19th century and a tea pot from this kiln and period is included in the exhibition (Exhibit 225).

中國陶瓷

中國陶瓷是世界主要造型藝術形式之一。在中國，開始燒造高溫陶瓷要比國外早很多個世紀。中國陶瓷蜚聲世界，因此，外國人稱中國爲China，意思便是「陶瓷之國」。燒成真正的瓷器需要超過攝氏一一八〇度以上的高溫。傳統看法認爲，中國約在公元十世紀時便已能燒達這個溫度，但自第二次世界大戰以來，人們提出的科學論據，證明最晚在東漢時已能燒至這個溫度。同時，把上限往上推至商代似乎也不無可能，要證實這一點也只是遲早問題而已。在西方，真正的瓷器要遲至公元一七〇〇年方始出現。

大多數自前代遺留下來的陶瓷都來自墓葬，數個世紀以來原封不動。自宋代開始，士大夫已大量蒐藏陶瓷珍品。佛教禪宗與茶道流行，傳至日本。因此，彼邦歷年來收集了不少精美的陶瓷，時至今日還遺存不少。

自古以來，陶瓷器均用作日常器具，例如煮食用的砵、盂、碟及水丞等。

中國陶瓷生產史大抵可以上溯至公元前六千年晚期，肇始自中原和西北部的甘肅省。新石器遺址中出土了大量陶器，部份還發現相當數量的玉器，這些陶瓷以紅坭爲胎，用坭條盤築法製造，把表面和裡面掃平使坭圈結合在一起以成形，接着塗上黑彩，有時還加上紅彩，繪上抽象或幾何圖案。這類陶器燒製的時期很早，公元前三千年已有燒造，因而產生了很多不同地方性類型的制品。這次展覽中便有幾件頗爲獨特的新石器時代陶器。第一件是仰韶文化馬廠期的雙聯罐，年代約在公元前三千年(展品1)。對於這種罐的用途的猜測饒有趣味，有人認爲或許是新石器時代舉行婚禮時的用品。第二件是在紅底上用黑彩畫有一個手持弓箭的人和一隊小鹿的罐(展品3)。這件器具來自中國西北部的青海省，屬卡若文化，年代約在公元前三千年晚期至公元前二千年早期。我相信這罐是獨一無二的。其他三件新石器時代陶器包括(a)罕有的龍山文化黑陶杯，這一件造型優美，胎薄，是典型的龍山陶器。製法是在陶輪上成形，與一般紅陶的造法不同(展品2)。山東省發現類似的陶器，年代相當於公元前二千五百年；(b)辛店文化彩陶罐，年代相當於公元前二千年晚期。此罐有長柄，是典型的辛店文化形狀，上繪有舞蹈人物，非常特別(展品4)；(c)齊家文化三脚盛器(展品5)。這件盛器的形狀與早商時期的銅祭器相似，所以我們可以肯定地把它的年代定爲商代早期，即是公元前二千年左右。

商代墓葬中埋藏着大量銅器，玉器、陶器、馬、姬妾、奴隸等。墓主的身份愈高則陪葬品的數量愈大。據已發表的發掘報告，商朝皇帝配偶婦好的墓中便發現數量極多的陪葬品。婦好卒於公元前一千四百年，從墓中物品便可知道中國貴族們的厚葬風氣。

以姬妾及奴隸殉葬的習俗到戰國時代已名存實亡，代之是木或陶製的俑。雖然在邊陲地方如南越，在漢代時仍有以姬妾和奴隸殉葬的風氣。前幾年在廣州發現了南越第二代皇帝的陵墓，這墓從未被盜和破壞。墓主死於公元前一二二年，其中便有用活人殉葬。以前用銅(展品7和9)和漆製造明器，至此亦爲陶器所代替。在漢代，陶製明器盛行，成爲一大行業，全國各地都有陶窯燒製。重要的漢墓中，仍然可以發現銅器、漆器、木器和陶器，但從前陪墓主殉葬的活人活馬在這個時期已經爲陶俑和陶馬所替代。

中國古代的陶窯數目甚多。一位有名的中國陶瓷專家對我說，他估計單是宋朝已最少有壹萬個窯場在進行生產。其中有些規模龐大，有些則畧小。由於窯場數目太多，所以即使根據目前的資料也很難確定某器所屬窯口，除非該器的胎身有其自身的特點，如建窯的紫坭(展品97)或磁州窯的灰中帶藍的胎身(展品74)，否則亦不容易辨別。一般來說，只能初步確認它是南方或北方窯的產品。有時，甚至連這一點也不能做到。至元代，陶瓷生產的地點趨向集中，而窯場亦趨於生產某些特定類型，從而使我們在考訂窯口時較爲容易。據說歐洲陶瓷也明顯地有相同現象：意大利的梅約里克瓷器，英國的德爾夫特瓷器便是典型的例子。由於生產的地方太多，所以往往難於決定某件陶瓷是哪個窯場的產品。

正如意大利的梅約里克瓷器和英國的德爾夫特瓷器一樣，以現今知識水平而言，要鑑定中國陶瓷的年代一般都沒有很大的困難，理由是某些造型和紋飾一旦在某地方流行，很快便會被各地的窯場爭相仿效。歐洲陶瓷的情況亦後一樣。工藝技術的突飛猛進像野火一般迅速傳播開去，導致成本減低，因而利潤增加。在美術史上，很少有論者會强調利潤這個因素。我以爲絕對有此必要。人們常常問我用甚麼準則來決定真僞的問題。一般來說，我是憑着學理和多年來累積的經驗。但還須考慮到現在的作僞者肯定不會花太多的時間，費很大的功夫去做一件令他蝕本的物品。因此，在鑑定時，利潤的動機也是一個重要的因素。

談到這裏似乎有必要舉例說明前述技術改進的情況。在唐朝以前，器物甚少有正式的圈足。六朝和初唐的器物通常都是實足，例如展品21。這時期要是發現有正式的圈足的話，便是因爲該類陶瓷模仿銅器的製作。假如銅器是實足的話，便會變得太重，在經濟上和美學上都不足取，因此要做成圈足。約在公元九世紀時，代替實足興起的是一種名爲「玉璧型」的底足。這種底足的形狀像一塊玉璧，素身無釉。展品37便是一個例子。這碗與一般玉璧底碗不同，它的足部滿釉，上有極細的支釘。在九世紀一些頗爲精細的白瓷和可能是模仿銅器形狀的陶器上可以見到另一種形式的底足。這種底足是在當時創製的，足頗闊，形畧方（展品32）。到公元十世紀，正式的圈足幾乎已廣爲各窯所採用，在此之前的玉璧型底足幾乎絕跡。據筆者所見，後期窯器具玉璧型底足的只有河南黑釉大罐，如展品75。這件的年代可能是在十一世紀，我認爲保留玉璧底足是因爲器身較大之故。正式的圈足的興起是技術上的一種進步，因泥的用量比實足爲少。起初，這種圈足傾於外撇（展品47），但至北宋早期，此特點似乎已經消失。

另一種創新的技術是採用級狀的匣砵以燒製一類口沿無釉的碗。這種方法可能是在公元十一世紀下半葉時肇自定窯。好處是能一次叠燒大量的成品，從而大大地減低成本。據説舊方法所需燃料的費用相當於全部製造費用的一半以上，因此新的技術迅即風行各地。但由於用級狀匣砵，致令器邊毛口，因此要用金屬包鑲（展品72）。

從中國藝術史家的觀點來看，最耐人尋味的現象是唐末時陶器器形的猝然改變。唐代陶瓷的瑰麗雄渾似被宋代典雅細膩的作風所取代，只有雄踞在北面與滿族人相類的遼王朝仍舊繼續生產唐代風格的陶瓷，如展品55。改變的原因未明，但很有可能是因爲茶道流行而茶道家倡議用較廉價的陶瓷器以取代昂貴的金屬和漆器。這種飲茶風氣在日本發展成爲日本茶道，那裏的茶道家特別喜愛樸實無華的陶瓷用具。宋代大規模的陶瓷外銷貿易也有可能是這種器形猝改的原因之一。碗形的改變起先是模仿金屬製品（展品44、51及52），從其本身來看，似乎已能證明導致這種改變必然是專爲取代金屬製品的緣故。

還值得一提的是有些窯場如磁州和西村窯，直至宋代還有模仿唐代銀器上的圈形地紋，這點足以證明陶瓷源自金屬器物的説法。展品50和61兩件磁州窯便是例子。隨着新技術的引進，如前述的級狀匣砵，宋代的碗形順應更改，變化愈大。

另一種工藝的革新是引進印花的技法。以模成形的方法至北宋已有很長的歷史，但用模子印成紋飾的方法則至北宋中期方始普遍。有些唐代陶瓷仿效波斯薩珊王朝或中國銀器，在器上印上花紋，但畢竟非常罕有，同時亦鮮有很成功的作品。展品38是晚唐時代的一件成功的例子。

在公元十一世紀中期以前，北宋陶瓷的紋飾通常是用刻花或拍壓方法製成，如展品54和56。印花的缺點是在上釉後不能呈現較清晰的圖案，這似乎需要在鍊泥和把泥坯剝離模范時格外小心，以免弄壞。準確掌握印花技術似乎是自十一世紀遼代控制下的定窯開始。展品60和70便是這類早期印花的好例子。展品60可能是定窯製造的遼代樣本，而展品70則與紀年公元一○五七年遼墓出土的一件碎片幾乎完全一樣。最先掌握印花技術的人是遼代陶工，這個看法還有以下的事實可以証明：高麗青瓷上的精美印花紋飾（有時甚至採用遼式花卉紋）似乎是自十二世紀二十年代開始出現，此時正值是遼代多事之秋，不久便於公元一一二五年滅亡。遼代陶工就在那時湧入高麗，使當地青瓷印花技術大爲提高。

早期的印花瓷器往往在脱模後，再加刻作爲修飾，因此有人在同一件器物上會見到刻花與印花同時存在（展品86）。到了南宋和金代，各地窯場流行印花，白釉和青白瓷大多採用這種技法（展品88，94和106）。只有青瓷仍用刻花的紋飾（展品138）。吉州窯似乎從來不用印花作爲裝飾，但卻用各種不同技法，如繪畫或剪紙，使紋飾更多采多姿（展品105，112和114）。

在宋代，某些窯場的産品的影響力很大，其它窯口都仿效其色澤、造型和紋飾，所以我們可以把整個組別大致定爲同一個年代。這些産品如定窯，其影響了十世紀和十一世紀的陶瓷工業、汝窯，它影響了十三世紀的陶瓷工業。因此，在鑑定這幾個世紀的陶瓷時不會有困難。流風所披，及於玉器、犀角雕刻和銅器，這些器物全部都可以在鈞窯産品，如碗和花盆找到例證。這次展覽中便有幾個例子（展品105和110）。有些在地域上非常接近的窯口也有相互的影響，如在江西省境內的贛州和吉州窯，兩者距離不遠。贛州窯燒造的所謂米量是典型當地産品（展品127）（按：可能實際上不是量米用具,而是與茶道有關的用具),吉州窰仿之,而典型的吉州窰釉卻又爲贛州窰所仿效(展品120)。

在漢墓出土的陶瓷中,大部份是敷綠色鉛釉的陶器,這種綠釉受侵蝕會出現銀白色(展品14)。有些是褐色鉛釉,但並非十分普遍。除鉛釉陶外,有些是無釉的陶瓷(展品9)或是在無釉的胎身上加上紅、黑、和白彩(展品13),有時還添加藍、綠和黃彩(展品10、11和12)。鉛釉陶似乎專爲陪葬而造。在東漢時期,富有的地主們用大量的陶俑、戰車、傭僕、附屬建築物如穀倉(展品17)、鴨池、豬屋、家禽之屬等陪葬,使他們宛似在生前一樣在巨大莊園中享用一切物品。我曾經見過一個豬圈的模型內有一隻疲乏的母豬正在分娩,一隻小豬正出娘胎,而其他的小豬則吮飲着母豬的乳汁。

屬日用品而不是陪葬品的早期釉陶可以分爲三大類:青釉、黑釉和白釉器。

含氧化亞鉄成份的高溫青釉器的歷史可以上溯至商代。至公元前九世紀,安徽和浙江省已能燒造數量頗大的青釉器。那時的產品常常有編纂的花紋。這次展覽中便有一件此類非常罕有的早期青釉器,它的釉上有藍白斑,這是因爲在燒製時木灰意外地落到釉面而形成(展品6)。這類窰器亦有用織物做成紋飾,如展品8。青釉器持續流行了幾百年,至東漢發展成爲早期的越窰。這種早期的越窰釉面光亮明淨。展覽中有一件越窰,年代約在東漢或稍後。在浙江上虞窰址出土的一些碎片與這件樣式一樣(展品16)。這次展覽中還有幾件越窰,年代約在公元三至四世紀(展品18及19)。這一類陶瓷在中國很多地方均有燒製,但主要產地是在浙江和廣東省。廣東的青釉器的支釘數目較浙江爲少(鮮有多個五個),同時似乎從未見到像浙江青釉器一樣在釉上加上褐斑的(參見展品18和19)。這一類越器與前期的不同所在,是自東漢時代開始燒製真正及實用的器具,而非像以前一樣,單單模仿銅器和漆器。

青釉器基本上不作陪葬用器,在唐以前差不多一直燒造,同時在製作技術方面有長足的進步。這些早期的越器後來發展成爲五代及北宋時的典型越窰(展品47和54),最後發展成爲典型的龍泉窰,如展品96及101。

在唐末、五代和北宋的青釉中最負盛名的是在五代末期和北宋初期吳國的產品。這類窰器在中國陶瓷史上稱爲「秘色窰」。長久以來,有人相信它是龍泉窰的

一種,也有人認爲它是越窰的一類,這個問題一直未能在考古學上予以確定。近年在陝西省扶風法門寺塔基發現了幾件精美的青釉器,埋藏的時間約在公元八六八至八七四年。這些青釉器在地基出土的手寫清單上稱爲「秘色窰」,因此可以確定它們無疑就是「秘色窰」,千古之謎,今天遂得解決。秘色窰實際上是質色俱精的上等越窰。有幾位香港收藏家最近到北京參觀了在法門寺出土的文物展覽,回來後告訴我展出的秘色窰器的釉和顏色與我收藏的一件綠鈞碟(展品64)一樣。可是越窰器的底部一般有一圈矽或砂痕(參見展品47和54),與鈞窰的燒製方法截然不同。因此,我認爲我的一件是北宋時代模仿秘色窰的優質綠鈞。不論碟形和無釉的方足均是典型的鈞窰風格,與越窰大不相同。綠鈞的開片釉通常有很強的光澤,這件則無,似乎是着意避免,以仿效秘色器。

與上述情況一樣,南宋初期的陶工特意仿效當時的高麗青瓷。太平老人在所著〈袖中錦〉書裏列舉「高麗秘色」和其他陶瓷爲「天下第一」。展品85的圓盒是一件精美的青釉器,可能是龍泉窰由出品,它模仿十二世紀上半葉的高麗青瓷。紋飾和顏色與一一二〇至一一五〇年間生產的上佳高麗青瓷非常相近,兩者不同的地方是後者是置於一圈矽或砂粒上,而在這個盒上則沒有此特徵。説來奇怪,〈袖中錦〉一書也提及定窰白瓷,但卻沒有提及其他青瓷,如汝窰和官窰(當今公認是當時出產所有青釉器中最精美的類型)。

自宋及元明幾朝,青釉器一直是中國陶瓷器中最重要的產品之一。此次展覽中便比較全面地揀選了一些青釉器,顯示這類陶瓷在其漫長的歷史上釉和風格的嬗變。宋代青釉器是在還原反應中燒成,釉中含有百分之一至二的氧化亞鉄。展覽中屬於這類型的陶瓷器還有官窰,藍色、紅色和帶斑的鈞窰與及仿鈞窰。鈞窰一般被納入青釉類別,因爲它亦是用氧化亞鉄作爲釉藥。展出的官窰器可能均爲龍泉窰的產品。該窰的產品與杭州的郊壇下官窰幾乎全無分別,唯一差異是龍泉窰的胎身似乎較爲密緻。筆者曾於一九八五年十一月到杭州的郊壇下官窰參觀新近發掘的文物。主管發掘工作人員告訴我截至目前爲止,考古發掘資料表明,所有以前被定爲修內司及郊壇下官窰型器都是郊壇下官窰的產品。由此引發出一個很重要的問題。這便是修內司官窰是否獨立存在的問題。文獻

資料似乎確認修內司窯的存在。一九九一年初，我在台北故宮博物館參觀了官窯展覽，其中便包括了這些所謂修內司官窯的窯器。我得承認我沒法把這些被標注爲修內司官窯的窯器與郊壇下官窯的產品分別開來。

我又獲悉南宋早期郊壇下官窯器的底足有類似汝窯的支釘痕，這點証實了傳統的說法，即郊壇下官窯的主要工匠實際上就是自北宋滅亡後隨宋室南遷的汝窯陶工。大部份官窯器都有同一特點：與胎身相對而言，釉表現得相當厚。展覽中有一件元代葫蘆形的小瓶，象耳部份釉質肥厚，幾至不能辨別其形狀（展品132）。

其次要討論的是黑釉器。這類窯器的色澤也是由氧化亞鐵而來，只不過黑釉器釉中的成份是在百分之七至百分之十之間，在還原反應中燒成。減少窯裡火膛的空氣，用還原焰可燒成黑釉器，如果增加火膛中的空氣則可燒成紅釉器。近年發現證明在東漢時代浙江上虞窯已開始燒製全身敷黑釉的器物，其中一些紋飾與展品16相似。起初黑釉器似乎與青色的早期越窯器在同一個窯內一起燒製，其後才成爲某些窯的特定出品。展品15是一件在越窯青釉上加上黑色和褐色寬帶的器物，年代屬東漢。它是青釉與黑釉結合的一件非常罕有的樣本。黑釉器自後很快成爲六朝早期浙江省德清窯的特產，而在當時生產的所有黑釉器中，最富特色的是雞頭壺，展覽中便有一件，可能是德清窯的產品（展品20）。近年發現一個紀年公元三七○年的墓，其中便有一件與以上這件相似的雞頭壺。

在晚唐之前，黑釉器似乎還不大流行，在八至九世紀時只有一類用磷酸鹽燒成帶藍白斑的黑釉器。這類器物往往具皮囊的特色，是目下收藏家所渴求的一種陶瓷器（展品30）。北宋時期黑釉器的產量陡然增加，風靡一時，究其因可能是晚唐及宋代之間，茶道流行，騷人墨客常加詠讚，加之其時佛教大盛，是以成爲宋代最流行的窯器之一，而且大量外銷到日本去。

在宋代，各地似乎都燒造黑釉器，但主要產地是在河南、江西、福建和河北幾省。

展覽的黑釉器包括罕有的定窯枕頭，其特色是輕、胎骨幼細（展品90）；河南窯枕頭，特色是重、粗糙，與定窯恰好相反（展品103）；罕有的陝西省耀州窯黑中帶紫色底鐵銹裝飾的碗（展品93）江西省的吉州窯和贛州窯；福建省的建窯；磁州窯；河南窯和山東各窯。值得一提的是吉州窯的葉紋碗（展品98）和來自吉州窯、

磁州窯、山東淄博窯的幾件紀年器（展品111、143和91）。在宋末和元代之間，陶工們常常在黑釉底上加上鮮明的金屬般的紅褐色紋飾（展品125和126）。

這次展覽中有幾件鐵銹釉器，包括兩件紫定碗（其中一件帶蓋）；耀州窯碗和晚明德化窯香爐（展品99、92、167）。日本人把這類滿蓋金屬性褐色，或鐵銹色的器具稱爲「柿天目」。有一位日本作者堅稱它們全是河南窯的產品。但我認爲這是不確的，因爲在燕山定窯窯址中發現了與展品99相同的紫定器；另一方面，河南窯、福建省的建窯都能生產柿天目。

河南窯這類窯器胎質粗，釉色暗黃（例如展品103）；福建省建窯的胎色則呈紫色或深褐色（例如展品97）；紫定的胎色是白中泛黃，映着燈光看來幾乎是透明一樣。耀州窯生產的鐵銹釉窯器在形狀和胎質方面均與該窯的其他產品相同（展品92和93）。磁州窯黑釉器的胎色往往呈明顯的灰藍色（展品74）。

黑釉器在元末以後似乎不再流行，碩果僅存的只有磁州窯，成爲唯一繼續生產黑釉器的主要窯場（展品143）。

另一類主要的早期中國陶瓷是白釉器。在這裏我把青白瓷也包括在內。這一類器物後期演進成爲精美的高温瓷器，在西方享有盛名。優質的白釉器似乎在公元六世紀、即六朝晚期時已經開始燒造。至唐末，茶道流行，同時人們喜愛用精美的瓷器作爲日用，遂導致白釉器的需求在唐代後期大爲增加。展品32和38是唐末的白釉器，其大抵是邢窯或定窯的產品，兩窯均位於河北省。

在伊拉克薩麻拉遺址中發現了數量甚多的白釉炻器碗，這些碗光素無紋，口沿厚突而底足像一塊玉璧，一般通稱薩麻拉型碗。邢窯和定窯兩窯均有生產這類樣式的碗，並大量外銷到其他國家去。薩麻拉位於今日的伊拉克境內，是古代一個重要中心，昌盛期約在公元八三八至八八三年。該地廢於八八三年，自後便無人居住，因此爲這類型碗提供了上佳的斷代條件，雖然我們不能排除它們在十世紀上半葉還有繼續燒造的可能。在1992年初，我終於確定了以上的看法。當時我在馬尼拉，一位古玩商給我看了幾個薩麻拉型碗。它們的玉璧形底足的一角被刀斜切去（這特點足以證明它們是定窯的產品，與它們相類的邢窯和鞏縣窯均沒有定窯的這個特點）；他又給我看了一個五代的白釉碗，但這件碗並沒有玉璧形底。在仔細觀察這個碗之後，我相信

它亦可能是定窯的產品。這位古玩商人細述這些碗全部來自菲律賓薩馬島同一個墓葬，發掘墓葬時他本人在現場，所以可以確定這些碗的發現地點和出處。早期的定窯最初生產類似這些薩麻拉型碗的素身白釉碗。鞏縣窯碗的風格也比較突出，就是它有外卷而非厚突的口沿。唐代青花瓷片便在此窯址發現。

公元十世紀時，北宋朝廷欽定定窯瓷為御器，從此愈益風行。

每當某種窯器開始流行，往往便會出現求過於供的情況，而其他窯場遂爭相仿效以圖分一杯羹。

在北宋，絕大部份的定窯產品都飾以精美的刻花圖案。但到金代則幾乎全為印花紋飾所取代。定窯產品如晚唐時的薩麻拉型碗本來是仿效邢窯，其後反過頭來變成是邢窯的模仿對象，展品88便一例。展品94是一件精美的金代典型定窯印花器，而展品95和124則是同一時代在山西省介休和霍縣模仿定窯的產品。

在眾多模仿者中，最有名的當然是景德鎮諸窯。約在公元一千年之前景德鎮已開始燒製白瓷。起初，它們企圖模仿定窯漂亮的黃白釉。但約在公元一千年以前，景德鎮陶工們便已有意識地並成功地燒成晶瑩可愛的天青色青白釉。在公元十一世紀前期，這種天青色釉似乎是鳳毛麟角，燒成也祇屬偶然而已。展品58、59和76代表了景德鎮諸窯在公元十一世紀前期及一一〇〇年前後的作品。前兩件的年代是公元十一世紀上半葉，而第三件則約是公元一一〇〇年。這些青白瓷是元代樞府窯、明清白瓷、元明清三代青花和其他晚期瓷器的先驅。景德鎮從此成為國內製造優質陶瓷的中心。名聞世界的「中國白」瓷器(譯者案:即國人稱為「福窯」的白釉瓷器)是在福建燒造的白瓷，是該省的特有產品。

展覽中展出公元九世紀至十八世紀的一系列白釉器，其中大部份是在景德鎮燒造，但前述的定窯白釉器、德化瓷(展品165和166)和其他瓷窯(展品43、45和48)亦一併展出。

除上述三大類外，還有彩瓷。這一類包括鉛釉或不是鉛釉的陶瓷。我指的是敷上超過一種釉色的窯器，而非在素胎加上彩色顏料一類。在唐代以前青釉上偶有加上鐵成份的褐斑(展品19)。至唐代這類青釉器仍在繼續燒造。名氣最大的早期彩器要算是唐三彩。它的釉是以鉛為基本成份，色澤有褐、綠及泛黃的白色(展品28)。這類絢麗的陶器似乎在公元七世紀已經開始燒製。除以上三個顏色外，稍後還添上藍色，但是極為罕有。至於在何時開始加入這種藍色則至目前仍未能確定。在一個紀年公元七二三年的墓中曾發現一件藍釉器，而在另一個紀年公元六六四年的鄭仁泰墓中據稱也發現一件，但可惜發掘報告頗為含糊不清。假如以上資料正確，有一點卻又使人迷惑，因為紀年公元七〇六年的永泰公主墓的眾多陪葬品中並沒有發現任何藍釉器;而在公元六六四年到七二三年的其他紀年墓中亦付闕如。三彩器在唐代非常流行，貴族們大量訂造。時至公元七五六年安祿山之亂和七六三年吐蕃入侵，數量始大為減低。而亦自這時開始，唐三彩的生產幾於停頓，後至公元十一世紀中葉遼代才得以復興。

展覽中有幾件標準的三彩器，其中一件帶藍釉，圖案用染纈法繪，年代可能是八世紀上半葉(展品28和29)。另一件是一個磁州窯枕，年代是十二世紀(展品87)。展品71和100是遼代的彩器。

唐代鉛釉陶器的製作過程中最重要的是在胎上加上一層白色陶衣。如果敷得均勻的話，燒成的釉便會十分漂亮(展品27)，反之則效果不佳。

中國陶工所採用的眾多技巧中，最有趣的要算是攪胎。攪胎是用不同顏色的陶泥揉捏在一起，待陶泥乾至如皮革般韌度時，刮去表層，接着把整件掛上透明的色釉，這些色釉一般是綠、褐和黃色。釉底下的不同顏色陶坯會令這件掛了釉的器物呈現大理石紋理的視覺效果。這類器物最先在中國唐代出現。展覽中便有兩件這類的褐釉和綠釉攪胎器(展品25和26)。自攪胎器出現後，衍生了幾種不同製法:一種是把攪好的坯切片，嵌在單一個顏色的陶坯上，然後掛釉;自唐中葉以降，這方法常常用於生產枕頭一類器物。第三種技法是在實心單色陶坯的底或邊上加上攪好的陶坯。最後這種方法似乎是在唐末才告出現，自後便成為一種通行的技法。展覽便有幾件第三類型的攪胎器，年代是自晚唐至北宋(展品36和72)。

攪胎器製作需要高度的技巧和複雜的工序，小心翼翼務使在刮坯時不會把坯混至模糊不清。因此在北宋時出現了仿攪胎的製作，方法是在單一顏色的胎身上用不同顏色的坯漿繪畫大理石紋，展品73便是這一類比較稀有的器物的樣本。北宋以後，攪胎器似乎不太流行，瀕於絕跡，只有在故意仿古的情況下才會燒造。

不用氧化鉛燒製彩器的方法最先在金代的磁州窑採用。幾乎所有的磁州窑器的燒造方法都甚為粗糙，呈灰或淡黄色的胎身上塗上一層白色陶衣，接着燒至一個較高的溫度，在釉上敷上各種氧化亞鐵色料，以較低溫度作第二次焙燒。燒成的釉上彩料的顏色初時有綠、黄、攀紅或黑色。對這些釉上彩料何時始燒的問題，過去的看法是在公元一二〇〇年之前不久的時間。但令我感到詫異的是我在巴黎塞魯斯基博物館見到一塊彩繪人物的碎片，說明稱它來自鉅鹿、或清河縣。這些市鎮在公元一一〇八年為長江泛濫所淹没，所以這類彩器的燒製年份似乎可能會比以前認為的年代更早。展品中有一件彩繪人物便屬這類彩器，非常罕有，年代在公元十三世紀（展品123）。這類釉上彩繪器在始燒後便一直受人歡迎，多個世紀以來，一直不衰。後來還漸漸加入了紫色。至清代，這種技法甚至超越了以前用鉛作為彩料的方法。展覽中還有另一些釉上彩器，其中一件是湖南省衡山窑（展品109），它與上述磁州窑彩繪人像約是同時代產品；另一些是明清的五彩器（展品150、155、158、179、183和184）。

在近年來發現的眾多值得玩味的瓷器類型中，有一類帶斑點的白釉器，紋飾方法是在白釉底下加上鐵銹斑點。在過去二十年間，印尼和菲律賓出土了很多在影青青白釉或青釉底下飾以褐斑的陶瓷器，這些都是我們相當熟悉的器物。展覽中便有年代屬南宋末年或元代的這類窑器（展品134和139）。在近幾年來發現了很多，它們也是用斑點作為裝飾的人像、動物和其他器物，但這類是蓋上白色泛黄、白色泛綠或早期影青的釉，而非像前者一樣蓋上藍色的青白釉。這組饒有趣味的陶瓷的產地至今還未能確定。一九六六年在景德鎮附近的一個墓中出土過這類型的器物，我相信該墓的年代為公元十一世紀上半葉。在景德鎮博物館肯定最少有一件屬於這類的器物。該館的館長認定該件的年份為北宋，但認為它不是景德鎮的產品。由於這類窑器的釉色白中泛黄，有別於南宋至元青白釉或樞府釉底下飾有褐斑的窑器（展品139），而明顯地與五代及北宋早期的白釉器的釉較為接近。這次展覽中有四件屬這些早期類型的器物（展品65、66、67和68）。南京博物館展出有一件素胎人首魚身像，被確定為五代，與展品66相似。

另一件值得玩味而同樣帶有斑點的器物是一件罕

有的鳳頭壺（展品53），年代可能是五代末期。這壺的鳳頭鐫刻精細，令人想起唐代的同類型壺。它與大英博物館藏的一件著名的壺相似，該件的年代被定為北宋。不同的是，該壺多了一圈模印團花裝飾，這類紋飾在北宋早期出口到菲律賓去的廣東窑器上可以見到。我收藏的一件沒有這圈紋飾，大致認定其為五代的產品，表明當時的出口還未像北宋一樣頻繁。論者認為大英博物館與展品53同是廣東潮州窑的產品。

其他特別的唐、五代和宋代的器物，包括一個唐陝西省耀州窑黑花小盒（展品34）、一組介休窑窑器（展品95、116和117）、渾源窑（展品42和104）、江西省南豐窑（展品121）。一九八〇年在英國牛津亞希莫林博物館和稍後在香港大學馮平山博物館展出的古窑址瓷片展覽中便有與以上幾件相類的窑器或碎片。山西省介休和渾源窑金代燒造的碗有一個特色，便是在碗心有一澀圈，是疊燒時遺留下來的痕跡。展品109是湖南省衡山窑的產品，在近期中國出版的一本書中便刊印有一件與它相似的碎片。

在晚期陶瓷方面，我特別注目於一些不大常見的類型，理由是在過去很多展覽中已多次展示過標準的明清窑器。這些特別類型包括一件不常見的明代素胎彩器（展品151）（譯者案：這裡指素三彩瓷器）、茄皮紫釉和紅釉的「金襴手」瓷器（展品152和153）、綠、黄和茄皮紫釉（譯者案：這也指素三彩瓷器）的兩個仙人像，它們附有鏤空底座，是作插香之用，與晚明的象牙製品可互為參照（展品164），此外另有一件帶青花和黑色的醬釉器（展品162）。

在清代瓷器方面，展覽中有一件精美的早期仿日本伊萬里瓷器（展品186）、一件仿布丁石紋的花盆（展品220）及兩件類型略有不同的爐鈞釉器（展品206和221）。

大約在公元一六八三年以前，彩器（譯者案：這裡指五彩瓷器）上的藍色大多是釉下藍色（案：即青花）（展品155和174）。但此後，釉上藍色流行，同時成為五彩瓷器上最主要的顏色之一。在一些晚期的明末清初交替瓷上也有用釉上的鈷藍色，但畢竟很少。據我所知，大英博物館藏有一件嘉靖款的瓷器，亦有釉上鈷藍色，是這類器物中最早的一件，也是唯一的一件。據說此物是十六世紀中葉的產品，但可惜我沒有見過。展品184是一件六角形的高足杯，為早期的五彩瓷器，敷有釉下和釉上兩種藍色。燒製在釉上加藍彩的五彩瓷器只需一次便可把所有釉上彩燒成，因而減少燒壞的可能,釉上藍彩的使用在公元一六八○年後開始流行。展品184上共用釉下和釉上藍色,表明其年份約在公元一六八五年前後。鬥彩瓷器要在白釉下繪畫藍色的款識或圖案的輪廓線,自然仍需在第一次燒製時達到攝氏一一八○度以上的溫度。另一件特別值得提及的是一個仿日本伊萬里的瓷器(展品186),這一件我相信可以認定爲公元一六九○年代末期的產品。在公元一六七七年至一六八三年間有三藩之亂,景德鎮瓷窯停頓,歐洲買家遂轉往日本訂購伊萬里和柿右衛門瓷器,由此大量輸入到歐洲並開始流行。典型的伊萬里色彩是以紅色(礬紅)爲主,釉下藍色,再潤飾以金彩。這類瓷器在公元一六九○年代初期原供歐洲宮廷之用,隨即風靡一時。除典型的伊萬里色彩外,展品186還具有幾處典型的日本特色,例如帶纓絡的族徽圖案,其中一個開光繪上標準伊萬里風格的菊石紋飾。這個花瓶異常精美,可以說工藝遠高於同期的日本伊萬里瓷器。因此我相信它是在伊萬里盛行後中國特意製造與日本爭一日長短的產品。

清朝燒造的瓷器爲數甚鉅,其中不乏精品。從工藝技術角度來看,雍正(公元一七二三至一七三五年)一朝的官窯瓷器可算是個中翹楚。很多評論家都認爲世界上再沒有其他地方的陶瓷可與之比擬。這次展覽選了幾件雍正朝的產品。展品196是一件顏色甚佳的釉裡紅瓷器。美麗的釉裡紅顏色是極難燒製的,成功的產品可以說是寥寥無幾。但雍正朝的陶工却能掌握燒製的技術并完全克服以往遇到的困難。在康熙早期,陶工們已經能夠成功地把釉裡紅與釉下青花一起燒成,同時取得漂亮的紅色。展覽中便有一件紀年公元一六七一年的釉裡紅青花瓷(展品175)。

清代最精良的瓷器是單色釉瓷,這是公認的事實。除沿襲以前各朝所有的單色釉如嬌黃(展品205)、甜白(展品190)、茶葉末(展品213)、官窯(展品212)、龍泉(展品214和215)繼續燒造之外,仿明青花器也是清代最精美產品之一(展品193、194和195)。這時又創燒或改良只有品種,如烏金、豇豆紅(展品192)、天藍(展品217)、深及淡茄皮紫(展品191和203)、蘋果綠(展品204)及郎窯(展品182)等。一九八五年十一月,我在景德鎮清代御窯遺址撿拾一塊盤子的碎片,與展品203幾乎完全相同。該遺址的所有建築在文革期間被破壞無存,只餘叢生雜草,堆滿精美破碎瓷片的山丘。

自公元一六八三年開始,清廷對景德鎮的御窯廠監管逐漸嚴格。尤其是在公元一七七○年後即乾隆中期時,陶工們嘗試燒製模仿其他質料如布丁石(展品220)和銅的瓷器。清中葉生產的釉色中,爐鈞釉是較爲特別的一種。雍正時爲草創期,而最後燒製成功則是在乾隆一代。這次展覽中有一件帶雍正款的樣本(展品206)。另有一件是綠色的爐鈞釉瓷器,帶乾隆款,是爐鈞釉的一種變體(展品221)。雍正的一件的釉色呈現不完全熔融狀態,與雍正朝一般的產品一致;而乾隆的一件的釉色則呈現已經完全熔融狀態,顯示當時已能成功地掌握燒製爐鈞釉的技術。

清代也有模仿前代的產品,例如鼎鼎大名的成化雞缸盃(展品189)。此外,亦有一部份仿效歐洲瓷器的花紋和顏色(展品207、209和210)。事實上,我們知道清廷耶穌會教士把歐洲利莫奇斯地方的琺瑯贈與清室的窯工,以燒製類似的琺瑯。已知傳世有六件仿利莫奇斯琺瑯的瓷器,明顯地源自耶穌會教士所提供的原作。這六件都寫有當地工匠Jacques Laudin(公元一六二七年至一六九五年)或他的同名侄子(公元一六六三至一七二九年)姓名的首個字母,在原作上無疑也有這兩個字母。中國所仿製的這一類的紋飾巧妙地把原作略爲改變。存世有兩件樣本的形狀相同,其中一件在這次展覽中展出(展品185),另一件則屬維多利亞艾伯特博物館的藏品。

清朝瓷器中有一類比較獨特的青花器(有時還與釉裡紅一起燒成),用淡描多於渲染的手法來描繪風格獨特的山石(譯者案:這種畫法有似中國山水畫技法中的「牛毛皴」,爲行文方便,就把這種畫法稱爲「牛毛皴」)(展品171和175)。有關這類瓷器的年代問題至今依然纏訟不休。中國學者堅持認爲是康熙晚期至雍正早期即約公元一七二○年間,而歐洲方面則認爲約在公元一六六○年至一六七五年間。這類瓷器的特點是用極細小的線條描繪山石。此外,以下幾種不同的邊飾也是常見的特徵:冰裂紋、松針紋或用濕筆繪畫的圓點紋。把「牛毛皴」一類瓷器確定爲公元一六六○至一六七五年現已普遍爲人接受。展品175和同類型瓷器帶有干支和年號款記,年代可準確定爲公元一六七一年,其他同類的帶有相似的款記的瓷器,其年代相當於公元一六七一年至一六七四年。根據這些瓷器,可以幫助解決這類瓷器的年代問題。

另一類明末清初交替瓷的年代在以前也有爭議，
這類便是繪有"V"字形草紋、偶帶干支款的瓷器（展品
168），歐洲的論者（指出公元一六六○年代的荷蘭風俗畫
上有相似的畫法）認爲其年代是在公元一六三六年至
一六四三年間。中國學者也堅持把這類的年代推遲
六十年。但約在去年，中國方面公開展出了一件繪有"V"
字形草紋的青花香爐，上有干支款和年代款，相當於公元
一六四○年，從而把這類瓷器的年代的問題解決，平息了
爭論。據我所見"V"字紋瓷器上最早的干支款是公元
一六二五年。記憶所及，我沒有見過干支款晚於一六五○
年的這一類器物。

　　自十八世紀開始，歐洲人在中國訂制帶族徽的
瓷器日漸增加，使得比較容易追溯訂制這類餐具的
家族的歷史。雖然自明朝嘉靖（公元一五二二至一五六六
年）已有燒造，但這類瓷器在十八世紀以前還是比較
罕見的。起初，只有葡萄牙家庭才擁有這類瓷器。
在公元一六○○年以前，葡萄牙人和西班牙人幾乎壟斷
了所有輸往歐洲的瓷器業務。但在一六○○年以後則
逐漸成爲荷蘭人的專利，這個情況維持到十七世紀
末葉，因而當時的族徽瓷器大多繪有荷蘭人家族的
徽號。在十八世紀，歐洲列强在廣州設廠的都紛紛
把瓷器運返本國。很多這個時期的族徽瓷器都是英國
家庭訂燒，展品215就是這一類餐具的精美樣本，
其年代是在公元一七二五年至一七五○年間。很多這類
餐具都是供英國巴斯地區的居民使用。一位族徽瓷器
專家現正居住在巴斯。近幾十年來，族徽瓷器成爲一種
專門的學問，融滙了有關中國瓷器與及紋章學和家系學
的知識。這類瓷器在公元一八五○年開始趨於衰微，十九
世紀所製的品質每況愈下。

　　一般陶瓷藝術論者都說十九世紀瓷器的質素要比
前代爲低。無疑，陶瓷的紋飾的確是趨於繁縟，但這種以
缺乏根據的說法却是欠妥的。中國在十九世紀時內亂
頻仍，國勢衰落。可是精美陶瓷的製作則從未間斷，
舉例來說，十九世紀初生產的宜興窰中便不乏佳作。
這次展覽中便有出自這時期的一個茶壺（展品225）。

Map showing approximate place in China of production of the wares mentioned in the text where known. 圖示記載於本書內在中國出產之陶瓷原産地

ZHEJIANG PROVINCE 浙江省

1. SHANGYU 上虞
2. NINGBO 寧波
3. DEQING 德清
4. YUYAO 餘姚
5. LONGQUAN 龍泉
6. JIAOTAN 郊壇

JIANGSU PROVINCE 江蘇省

7. YIXING 宜興

FUJIAN PROVINCE 福建省

8. DEHUA 德化

GUANGDONG PROVINCE 廣東省

9. CHAOZHOU 潮州
10. XICUN 西村
11. SHIWAN 石灣

JIANGXI PROVINCE 江西省

12. NANFENG 南豐
13. JINGDEZHEN 景德鎮
14. GANZHOU 贛州
15. JIZHOU 吉州

HUNAN PROVINCE 湖南省

16. CHANGSHA 長沙
17. HENGSHAN 衡山

HEBEI PROVINCE 河北省

18. DING 定窯
19. CIZHOU 磁州

HENAN PROVINCE 河南省

20. GONGXIAN 鞏縣
21. MIXIAN 密縣
22. DENGFENG 登封
23. JUNYAO 鈞窯
24. LUSHAN 魯山
25. RUYAO 汝窯

SHANDONG PROVINCE 山東省

26. ZIBO 淄博

SHAANXI PROVINCE 陝西省

27. YAOZHOU 耀州

SHANXI PROVINCE 山西省

28. JIEXIU 介休
29. HUOXIAN 霍縣
30. HUNYUAN 渾源

CHRONOLOGY 年表

			公元前 B.C.
NEOLITHIC PERIOD 新石器時代			*c.* 7000 — 2000
XIA 夏			*c.* 2100 — 1600
SHANG 商			*c.* 1600 — 1100
ZHOU 周			*c.* 1100 — 256
	Western Zhou 西周		*c.* 1100 — 771
	Eastern Zhou 東周		770 — 256
		Spring and Autumn period 春秋時期	770 — 475
		Warring States period 戰國時期	475 — 221
QIN 秦			221 — 206
HAN 漢			206 — 公元 A.D. 220
	Western (Former) Han 西（前）漢		206 — 公元 A.D. 8
	Xin (Wang Mang) 新（王莽）		公元 A.D. 9 — 25
	Eastern (Later) Han 東（後）漢		公元 A.D. 25 — 220

				公元 A.D.
SIX DYNASTIES 六朝				220 — 589
	Three Kingdoms period 三國			220 — 280
	Wu 吳		220 — 280	
	Shu 蜀		221 — 263	
	Wei 魏		220 — 265	
	Western and Eastern Jin 西晉東晉		265 — 420	
	Period of Northern and Southern dynasties 南北朝時代			386 — 581
	North 北朝	Northern Wei 北魏	386 — 534	
		Eastern Wei 東魏	534 — 550	
		Western Wei 西魏	535 — 557	
		Northern Qi 北齊	550 — 577	
		Northern Zhou 北周	557 — 581	
	South 南朝	(Liu) Song （劉）宋	420 — 479	
		Southern Qi 南齊	479 — 502	
		Liang 梁	502 — 557	
		Chen 陳	557 — 589	
SUI 隋				581 — 618
TANG 唐				618 — 906
	High Tang 盛唐			684 — 756
	Late Tang 晚唐			757 — 906

FIVE DYNASTIES 五代			907 — 960
LIAO 遼			907 — 1125
SONG 宋			960 — 1279
	Northern Song 北宋	960 — 1127	
	Southern Song 南宋	1127 — 1279	
JIN 金			1115 — 1234
YUAN 元			1279 — 1368
MING 明			1368 — 1644
	Hongwu 洪武	1368 — 1398	
	Jianwen 建文	1399 — 1402	
	Yongle 永樂	1403 — 1424	
	Xuande 宣德	1426 — 1435	
	Zhengtong 正統	1436 — 1449	
	Jingtai 景泰	1450 — 1457	
	Tianshun 天順	1458 — 1464	
	Chenghua 成化	1465 — 1487	
	Hongzhi 弘治	1488 — 1505	
	Zhengde 正德	1506 — 1521	
	Jiajing 嘉靖	1522 — 1566	
	Longqing 隆慶	1567 — 1572	
	Wanli 萬曆	1573 — 1620	
	Taichang 泰昌	1620	
	Tianqi 天啟	1621 — 1627	
	Chongzhen 崇禎	1628 — 1644	
QING 清			1644 — 1912
	Shunzhi 順治	1644 — 1661	
	Kangxi 康熙	1662 — 1722	
	Yongzheng 雍正	1723 — 1735	
	Qianlong 乾隆	1736 — 1795	
	Jiaqing 嘉慶	1796 — 1820	
	Daoguang 道光	1821 — 1850	
	Xianfeng 咸豐	1851 — 1861	
	Tongzhi 同治	1862 — 1874	
	Guangxu 光緒	1875 — 1908	
	Xuantong 宣統	1909 — 1912	
REPUBLIC OF CHINA 中華民國			1912
PEOPLE'S REPUBLIC OF CHINA 中華人民共和國			1949

THE
EXHIBITS

1

PAINTED DOUBLE CUP

NEOLITHIC, MACHANG CULTURE
 (*circa* 2500 B.C.)
WIDTH : 19.7 CM
HEIGHT : 8.3 CM

Double cup joined by a hollow tube at the base so that liquid can
go from one cup to the other. A strap handle painted with black and
red bands joins the lip and the lower body of both cups. The black
band consists of quartered square windows in reserve with central
dots. This pattern is repeated six times on the body and round the
lip on each cup and once on each side of the connecting tube.

2*

BLACK BEAKER

NEOLITHIC, LONGSHAN CULTURE
SHANDONG PROVINCE
  (*circa* 2500 B.C.)
HEIGHT : 14 CM
WIDTH AT WIDEST SECTION : 9.2 CM
WIDTH OF MOUTH : 4.8 CM
WIDTH OF BASE : 4.4 CM

An undecorated black beaker of typical very thin construction, the
interior showing signs of having been formed on a potter's wheel,
waisted two thirds of the way down from rim to base. Solid base. A
similar beaker has been excavated in Shandong Province from
late-early to early-middle Longshan levels dating to *circa* 2500 B.C.

3

OCHRE-RED JAR WITH DEER
AND ARCHER

NEOLITHIC, KARUO CULTURE
QINGHAI PROVINCE
 (*circa* 2300 - 1800 B.C.)
HEIGHT: 14 CM
WIDTH : 12 CM

Jar with two small handles, covered with ochre-red coloured pigment
down three quarters of the exterior and about 1.3 cm into the interior.
Painted in black on handles and inside the rim with chevrons, a band
of chevrons with lines round the jar under the handles. The middle of
the jar has a continuous band of deer of different sizes and sexes and
a man with bow and arrow all drawn in black pigment on the
ochre-red ground. The pottery of brick-red colour, the base with
shallow indentation.

4

DOUBLE-HANDLED BEAKER WITH DANCING FIGURES

LATE NEOLITHIC, XINDIAN CULTURE
 (*circa* 2000 - 1500 B.C.)
HEIGHT : 20.3 CM
WIDTH : 12.0 CM

A painted beaker with long handles from lip to half way down the body, the vertical panels on each side formed by triple vertical lines and two undulating triple lines at the bottom of the vertical panels. The handles and vertical panels are each decorated with a stylised kilted standing figure, all in black pigment.

5

TRIPOD *LI* JAR WITH
INCISED DECORATION

LATE NEOLITHIC, QIJIA CULTURE
QINGHAI PROVINCE
SHANG DYNASTY
  (*circa* 1800 - 1500 B.C.)
HEIGHT : 18.7 CM
WIDTH : 15.2 CM

Tripod *li* jar of light brick-red clay, the mouth slightly thickened
with one strap handle from just under the mouth rim to the top of
one leg, the hollow legs decorated with numerous finely incised-
line chevron patterns.

6

GREEN-GLAZED GREY POTTERY
WATER CONTAINER

WESTERN ZHOU DYNASTY
  (10TH TO 8TH CENTURY B.C.)
DIAMETER : 10 CM
HEIGHT : 5 CM

A small grey pottery water container with wide mouth, slightly
concave base and protruding shoulders. The shoulders are
decorated with zig-zag simulated weave pattern and applied with
three horizontal S-shaped ornaments while the base is carved with
a three stroke H-like incision. The container is covered with a
primitive brownish-green iron oxide glaze with an accidental
phosphatic splash caused by wood ash splashing onto one shoulder
during firing. Similar pieces have been excavated from Tunxi,
Anhui Province and Quzhou, Zhejiang Province.

7*

THREE-LEGGED POTTERY VESSEL
IN THE SHAPE OF A BRONZE *HE* KETTLE
WITH COVER AND HIGH HANDLE,
DECORATED WITH BANDS OF S STAMPINGS
COVERED WITH A RICH BROWN GLAZE,
THE SPOUT IN THE FORM OF A TWO-
HORNED STYLISED DRAGON'S HEAD

EARLY WARRING STATES PERIOD
  (LATE 5TH OR EARLY 4TH CENTURY B.C.)
OVERALL HEIGHT : 26.7 CM
WIDTH : 24.1 CM
THE COVER
HEIGHT : 6.4 CM
WIDTH : 9.5 CM

Three-legged pottery vessel in the shape of a bronze *he* kettle. The spout has a two-horned stylised dragon's head with a high handle on the back of which appear appliques which could represent the tail of the dragon. The body of the vessel is stamped with two bands of horizontal Ss and two bands of vertical Ss, and two simulated ring appliques at right angles to the handle on either side of the mouth. The round domed cover with pointed finial is stamped with similar S bands and one band of straight vertical lines; the vessel and cover have a rich brown glaze pooling in places.

8

GREEN-GLAZED GREY
POTTERY JAR IMPRESSED
WITH CLOTH PATTERN

WARRING STATES PERIOD
  (*circa* 4TH CENTURY B.C.)
DIAMETER : 9 CM
HEIGHT : 7 CM

A small, thinly potted grey-bodied jar of globular shape and wide mouth. The sides of the jar are attached with a pair of long S-shaped strap handles which extend up to the level of the mouth; each is topped with horizontal S-shaped appliques. The body is decorated with an imprint of textile fabric. The top part is covered with dark blackish-green glaze.

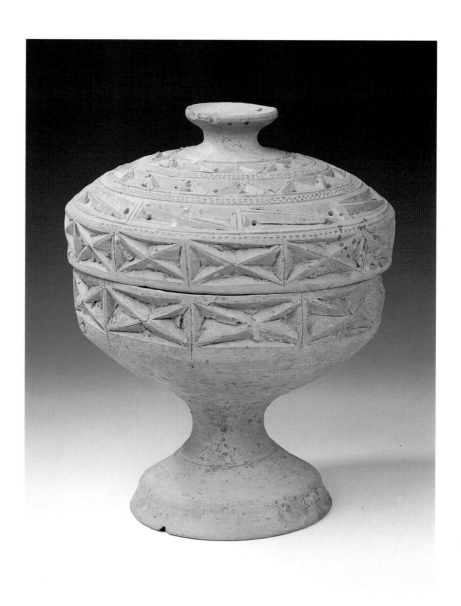

9

GREY UNGLAZED POTTERY COVERED *DOU*

LATE WARRING STATES TO EARLY
WESTERN HAN DYNASTY
 (3RD TO 2ND CENTURY B.C.)
HEIGHT : 22.5 CM
DIAMETER : 18.3 CM

An unglazed grey pottery *dou*, the body and cover decorated with deeply carved bands of cross pattern as well as zig-zag decoration with numerous holes. Probably for holding steamed food. A similarly decorated pottery piece was found in the early Western Han, Mawangdui burial *circa* 162 B.C.

10

PAINTED GREY POTTERY *HU* VASE WITH CLOUD DESIGN AND COVER

WESTERN HAN DYNASTY
  (2ND CENTURY B.C.)
HEIGHT : 43 CM
DIAMETER : 33 CM

A painted Han pottery vase and cover imitating the shape of a bronze *hu* vase. The vase has a dark grey globular body, high ring foot and dome-shaped lid. Two monster masks with rings and concave bands in pottery relief are applied on the shoulder. The neck and body are decorated with cloud patterns painted in red, white and indigo blue.

11

PAINTED GREY POTTERY JAR WITH CLOUD AND DISSOLVING DRAGON DESIGN

WESTERN HAN DYNASTY
 (LATE 2ND CENTURY B.C.)
HEIGHT : 35.6 CM
WIDTH : 25.4 CM

A grey pottery circular *hu*-shaped jar painted over a black slip with a lacquer type design of clouds and dissolving dragons in white, green, orange and red pigments, red being the predominant colour. The two monster masks holding the ring handles are in solid, deep red clay relief, but with the horizontal bands and ring handles just painted. This feature suggests a slightly later dating than Exhibit 10.

12

Painted pottery tortoise lamp

Western Han dynasty
 (late 2nd to 1st century B.C.)
Length : 16.5 cm
Height : 14 cm
Diameter of the tray : 11.4 cm
Width : 11 cm

A painted grey pottery tortoise lamp or *tazza,* the carapace covered by circular pimples in low relief, each with a central boss. The back has a central pillar surmounted by a circular tray. The grey pottery is covered with a white slip and the carapace is over-painted with lilac blue. The circular tray has traces of red clouds painted on the white slip on its vertical sides.

13

PAINTED MALE DANCING FIGURE

EARLY EASTERN HAN DYNASTY
  (1ST CENTURY A.D.)
HEIGHT : 35.5 CM
WIDTH : 24 CM

A grey pottery male figure with small black cap in dancing posture.
He wears a long robe, which covers the feet except for the tip of his
left shoe. The robe is painted with white pigment while the collar
is painted red. The eyebrows and eyes are highlighted in black and
the lips in red.

14

GREEN LEAD-GLAZED POTTERY LADLE WITH DRAGON'S HEAD HANDLE

EASTERN HAN DYNASTY
  (1ST OR 2ND CENTURY)
THE LADLE 8 CM FROM TIP TO HANDLE
LENGTH : 14 CM
HEIGHT OVERALL : 11.4 CM
DEPTH : 3.8 CM

A pottery ladle of deep oval tear-shape with handle ending in a
dragon's head, its mouth partly open. The bottom of the ladle has a
complex pattern of swirling lines in low relief, covered all over
with a thick, dark green lead glaze with three spur marks showing
the red clay body.

15

CIRCULAR YUE STONEWARE
HU-SHAPED VASE WITH THREE
BLACK BANDS

EASTERN HAN DYNASTY
 (1ST CENTURY)
HEIGHT : 34.9 CM
WIDTH : 22.9 CM

Circular *hu*-shaped pottery vase of hard reddish buff clay, of
traditional shape but with three raised bands on the shoulder, the
neck with incised wavy bands and unglazed. It is glazed in the
interior and down to the lower band with a deep sea-green iron
oxide glaze of Yue type. The three bands are accentuated with a
thick brown suffused black glaze, the two chevron-decorated
handles joining the upper two black bands, topped by stylised
ram's horn appliques. The deliberate use of black glaze here makes
this one of the earliest examples of its kind. This glaze is also
derived from iron oxide but in higher concentration than on the
celadon pieces.

16
CIRCULAR YUE STONEWARE VASE WITH IMPRESSED DESIGN

SHANGYU KILN, ZHEJIANG PROVINCE
EASTERN HAN DYNASTY
  (2ND OR EARLY 3RD CENTURY)
HEIGHT : 26.7 CM
WIDTH : 26.7 CM

Circular *hu*-shaped stoneware vase, the mouth rather saucer-like and decorated on its exterior with a thickened circular ridge band, the very short neck decorated with two closely impressed bands, its two strap handles with herringbone relief decoration and its bulbous body stamped with many basket-like decorative squares, all covered with a greyish-green iron oxide glaze of Yue type. Sherds of identical design dated to Eastern Han from the 2nd or early 3rd century A.D. from the Shangyu kiln, Zhejiang Province were included as Exhibit 6 in the Kiln Sherds Exhibition at the Ashmolean Museum in 1980.

17

BRICK-RED POTTERY HOUSE

LATE EASTERN HAN DYNASTY
  (EARLY 3RD CENTURY)
LENGTH : 31 CM
HEIGHT : 26 CM
WIDTH : 21 CM

A brick-red pottery verandahed house with a single set of grooved roof tiles at the back and two overlapping sets of grooved roof tiles in the front. The sides are decorated with five or six differently shaped holes for ventilation. The front door is flanked by pillars topped by typical *dougong* bracket sets supporting the eaves. The verandah wall is also decorated with six openings on each side. The unusual overlapping of the front roof tiles dates this piece to the late Eastern Han *circa* 200-220 A.D.

18

YUE VASE WITH FOUR CIRCULAR LOOPS ON SHOULDERS

WESTERN JIN DYNASTY
  (3RD TO 4TH CENTURY)
HEIGHT : 30.5 CM
DIAMETER : 21.8 CM

A Yue stoneware vase with flat everted mouth rim and broad
shoulders, the latter applied with two pairs of circular double-loop
handles and decorated with two bands of incised lines. The body is
covered with a yellowish-green glaze down about three quarters of
the surface of the exterior with occasional accidental brown spots.
The brown spots indicate this vase is probably from a Zhejiang
Province kiln.

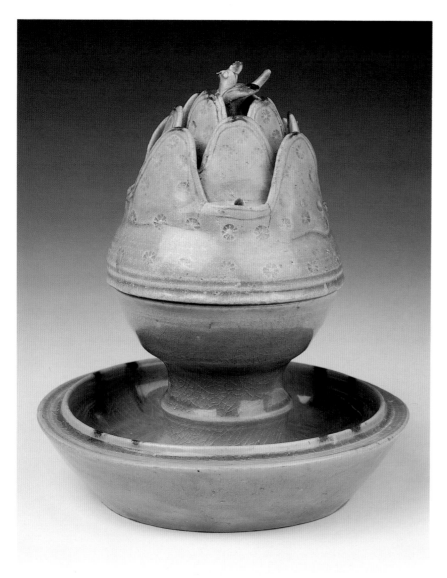

19

YUE BROWN-SPOTTED BOSHANLU
CENSER WITH BIRD FINIAL

LATE WESTERN JIN DYNASTY
 (*circa* 300 A.D.)
HEIGHT OVERALL : 20.3 CM
DIAMETER OF BASE : 16.5 CM
HEIGHT OF BASE : 11.4 CM

Yue brown-spotted Boshanlu censer, the plain base section a
heavily potted deep saucer with an inner ridge, the incense
container sits on a pedestal, the cover with three rings of four
stylised petalled mountain peaks each hiding one circular aperture,
the extreme top surmounted by a small bird. The whole cover is
covered by a yellowish glassy celadon glaze of Yue type with brown
spots, the cover also impressed with stars under the glaze. From a
Zhejiang Province kiln, possibly the Shanglinhu kiln.

20

CHICKEN-HEADED EWER WITH BLACKISH-BROWN GLAZE

DEQING OR YUHANG KILN
ZHEJIANG PROVINCE
EASTERN JIN DYNASTY
 (4TH CENTURY)
HEIGHT : 26 CM
DIAMETER : 20 CM

A large chicken-headed ewer with two square lugs on the shoulders, covered with dark blackish-brown glaze. Probably from the Deqing or Yuhang kiln of Zhejiang Province. A similar ewer has been excavated from a tomb dated 365 A.D. The square lugs are typical of the period and contrast with the use in the preceding century of circular loops (see Exhibit 18).

21

YUE COVERED DISH WITH LOTUS PATTERN

SOUTHERN DYNASTIES PERIOD
  (6TH CENTURY)
DIAMETER : 15 CM
HEIGHT : 7.6 CM

A Yue covered dish, probably for cosmetics, the cover of which is moulded in relief as lotus petals with a knob in the shape of a small lotus pod. The bottom section with a solid base is also carved in the shape of an open lotus flower with a shallow tray in the centre. The whole dish is covered with a thick, transparent, glassy, crackled, yellowish-green glaze typical of the period and its southern provenance.

22

DATED BUFF POTTERY STANDING
FIGURE OF AVALOKITESVARA

NORTHERN QI DYNASTY
  (563 A.D.)
HEIGHT : 22.5 CM
SIDES OF SQUARE PLINTH : 6.5 CM
WIDTH : 4.6 CM

Buff pottery standing figure of Avalokitesvara with elaborate crown
and pointed *mandorla* festooned with sausage-like necklace pendants,
the right arm bent at the elbow, its hand raised and the other arm
hanging down. The clothes, with long pendant draperies, cover the
thin match-stick like legs, and the feet and ankles are of almost
upright triangular shape, both features typical of the Buddhist
bronzes and marble statues of the period from Northern Qi to early
Sui (*circa* 550 - 590A.D.). The figure ends in a ceramic plug which
fits into a circular inverted lotus petal stand on a square plinth. The
reverse of the figure has a dated dedicatory inscription in black ink
dating the figure to the 5th day of the 10th Moon of 563 A.D..

23

TORTOISE-SHAPED FLASK WITH BROWNISH-GREEN TEA-DUST GLAZE

SIX DYNASTIES TO EARLY TANG DYNASTY
 (6TH OR 7TH CENTURY)
HEIGHT : 30 CM
WIDTH : 26 CM

A flat round stoneware flask in the shape of a tortoise; its stylised
head forming the opening, its front legs forming a pair of handles;
the brownish-coloured body covered on the upper half with a
brownish-green glaze of tea-dust colour.

24

BROWN LEAD GLAZED *WAN NIAN* JAR

TANG DYNASTY
 (7TH OR 8TH CENTURY)
HEIGHT : 15.2 CM
WIDTH : 12.5 CM

A brown lead-glazed circular *wan nian* (myriad years) jar with high
shoulders, the mouth with everted lip, the brown glaze extending
almost to the solid base, the body of pinkish clay. Probably from a
Henan kiln.

25

GREEN MARBLED WARE
TRIPOD JAR AND COVER

TANG DYNASTY
  (HIGH TANG 684 - 756 A.D.)
HEIGHT : 6.3 CM
WIDTH : 5.7 CM

A three-legged globular pot of typical Tang shape and of small size,
the legs ending in well modeled lion's feet, the body of dark and
light brown and white marbled clay throughout, covered by a thin
green glaze, a small cover of similarly glazed marbled ware. The
mixing of three different coloured clays rather than two colours is
unusual.

26

A BROWN MARBLED WARE
OFFERING TRAY

TANG DYNASTY
 (HIGH TANG 684 - 756 A.D.)
DIAMETER : 12.7 CM
DEPTH : 2.2 CM

A marbled ware offering tray on three small stubby legs. The clay
is of brick and buff colour covered on top and over the rim with a
dark yellowish-brown glaze, three spur marks on the top, the tray
with narrow flat rim and thickened edge. Probably made at a
Loyang kiln, Henan Province, where sherds of similar marbled
ware pieces have been found.

27

TRIPOD JAR WITH LION'S FEET COVERED BY GREEN LEAD GLAZE

TANG DYNASTY
 (HIGH TANG 684 - 756 A.D.)
DIAMETER : 8 CM
HEIGHT : 7.5 CM

An earthenware jar on three legs ending in lion's feet, covered with a splashed green lead glaze with white spots over a white slip.

28

SANCAI GLAZED POTTERY FIGURE OF AN OFFICIAL OF KHOTANESE TYPE

TANG DYNASTY
 (HIGH TANG 684 - 756 A.D.)
HEIGHT : 71.1 CM
WIDTH : 16.5 CM

A glazed pottery figure of an official of Khotanese type, standing on a plinth splashed with *sancai* buff, green and chestnut glaze, his hands clasped and concealed beneath a chestnut coloured muff, wearing a high necked jacket with wide pendant sleeves, the back swayed; all with typical *sancai* lead glazes of buff, chestnut-brown and green hue, the pixie hat with turned up ear flaps unglazed other than on a hawk applique which is splashed in chestnut-brown. The unglazed face with severe expression and traces of red pigment remaining on the lips and traces of black pigment depicting eyebrows and moustache.

29

Sancai JAR WITH STYLISED
WAX-RESIST FLORAL AND
GEOMETRIC PATTERNS WITH
BLUE GLAZE ADDED TO THE
SANCAI PALETTE

TANG DYNASTY
  (1ST HALF OF THE 8TH CENTURY)
DIAMETER : 17 CM
HEIGHT : 7 CM

An earthenware jar with wide mouth, globular body and a pair of
loop handles in the shape of double gourds; the upper part of the
exterior is decorated with stylised wax-resist floral and geometric
patterns in brown, blue and green lead glazes on a white ground
over a white slip. The interior is covered with a buff glaze.

30

BLACK GLAZED EWER WITH BLUE PHOSPHATIC SUFFUSIONS

PROBABLY LUSHAN KILN
HENAN PROVINCE
TANG DYNASTY
  (8TH OR 9TH CENTURY)
HEIGHT : 25 CM
DIAMETER : 15 CM

A stoneware *huangdao*-type ewer with a short circular spout and double-strap studded handle inspired by a leather original, covered with a thick black glaze with extensive pale bluish phosphatic suffusions, the lower portion and base are unglazed showing the greyish-brown body and solid knife-parred foot.

31

OX-DRAWN COVERED WAGON
WITH LADY PASSENGER
COVERED WITH DARK BROWN
AND WHITE GLAZE

LATE TANG DYNASTY
 (9TH CENTURY)
HEIGHT : 11.2 CM
LENGTH : 8 CM
WIDTH : 4.7 CM

A stoneware model of a covered wagon drawn by a yoked oxen attended by a peasant with a lady seated inside. The roof of the wagon, peaked at both ends, is glazed dark brown with two floral embellishments, the wheels and other small details on the ox and figures are dotted with brown and covered with a greenish-white translucent glaze. A similar wagon has been excavated from a mid 9th century tomb in Henan Province.

32

DEEP, WHITE-GLAZED
PORCELANEOUS BOWL
WITH EVERTED RIM

NORTHERN WHITE WARE
TANG DYNASTY
 (9TH CENTURY)
DIAMETER : 17.8 CM
DEPTH : 6.4 CM

A deep, white-glazed porcelaneous bowl with everted rim, the
base with squared foot-rim, the outer edge of the foot-rim vertical,
the inner edge of the foot-rim concave. The bowl (other than the
base and foot-rim) covered with a pleasant white glaze of creamy
tone, the body of fine white clay; either Ding or Xing ware.

33

CHANGSHA WATER POT
IN THE SHAPE OF A
MYTHICAL ANIMAL

TONGGUAN KILN
LATE TANG DYNASTY
 (SECOND HALF OF THE 9TH CENTURY)
HEIGHT : 5.5 CM
LENGTH : 6 CM

A Tongguan Changsha water container in the form of a fat dog-like animal with wide open mouth forming the spout and a ringed handle on its back. The upper half of the body is covered with a greenish glaze with underglaze brown and green stripes. The lower part is unglazed revealing the greyish-brown body.

34

Yaozhou circular covered box with formal black pattern

Late Tang dynasty
 (9th century)
Diameter : 5.1 cm
Depth : 3.2 cm

A circular box with convex cover and straight sides, the base solid with a knife-parred section round the base, the top with brownish-black dots and splashes forming a stylised pattern all on a thin white slip, the base unglazed revealing a putty coloured body. The cover of a similar box from the Yaozhou kiln site was included as Exhibit 438 in the Kiln Sherds Exhibition at the Ashmolean Museum in 1980.

35

ZHADOU JAR WITH BROWN *ZHADOU* PATTERN

LATE TANG DYNASTY
  (9TH CENTURY)
DIAMETER OF MOUTH : 11 CM
HEIGHT : 9 CM

A jar of whitish-coloured clay in the shape of a *zhadou* or slops container, covered with four large matt brownish-black splashes echoing the shape of the jar over a white slip. The solid foot is of broad *bi*-type with pared edge. The decoration echoing the shape of the jar itself is surprising and aesthetically pleasing.

36

MARBLED WARE CUP WITH FACETED RING HANDLE

LATE TANG DYNASTY
 (9TH CENTURY)
DIAMETER : 7.5 CM
HEIGHT : 5.4 CM

A small brown and white marbled earthenware cup with a
five-faceted handle, covered both inside and out with a brown glaze.
The base and shallow foot-ring is of unmarblized reddish clay.

37

YELLOW BOWL WITH *BI* FOOT

LATE TANG DYNASTY
 (9TH CENTURY)
DIAMETER : 16.5 CM
DEPTH : 4.4 CM

A high-fired bowl of shallow form, the *bi*-type foot of flat wide form has a small shallow indentation on the base. The entire bowl, including the base, is covered with a lead glaze of dark, streaky straw-yellow colour, the foot has traces of five very fine spur marks. Potted in two firings, the body and the glaze being separately fired.

38

TREFOIL BOX WITH BUSHY-TAILED FOX APPLIQUE

NORTHERN WHITE WARE
LATE TANG DYNASTY
  (9TH OR EARLY 10TH CENTURY)
LENGTH : 7.6 CM
WIDTH : 5.1 CM
HEIGHT : 3.6 CM

A covered box of trefoil shape copying a Tang silver box shape, the cover moulded as a convex lotus leaf with raised double line edges, the centre has an outstretched bushy-tailed fox applique covered with white glaze and delicately potted. The foot, base and central section of the sides unglazed. Either from the Xing or Ding kiln, probably the former.

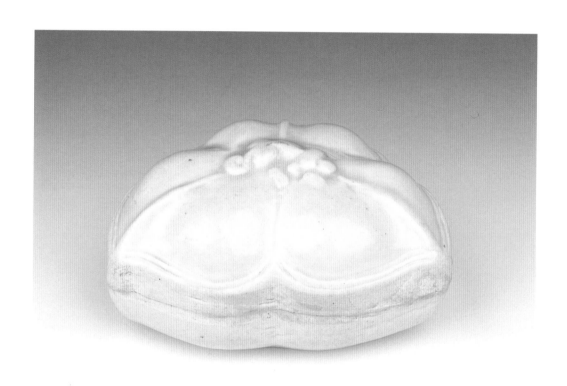

39

YUE CELADON JAR WITH
MANDARIN DUCKS AND
LOTUS MEDALLIONS

LATE TANG DYNASTY
 (9TH OR 10TH CENTURY)
WIDTH : 10.2 CM
HEIGHT : 7.6 CM

A globular Yue jar on a relatively high outsplayed foot decorated
under a rather glassy blue-green celadon glaze with four incised
circular medallions formed by four lotus leaves, and four buds and
stems joining the leaves, each medallion with a mandarin duck
standing up with wings outstretched. The borders around the mouth
are incised with scrolls as is the decoration separating the medallions.

40

HIGH-FOOTED CIZHOU
ALTAR OFFERING BOWL

LATE TANG TO FIVE DYNASTIES PERIOD
 (10TH CENTURY)
WIDTH : 12.9 CM
HEIGHT : 8.6 CM

A high-footed altar offering bowl with nearly flat everted mouth
rim and widely splayed high foot. The grey stoneware body is
covered with a white slip with green splashes in the glaze, covered
by a transparent glaze stopping short of the base. A horizontal
flange with wavy piecrust edge encircles the lower part of the
bowl, the main section has moulded and applied Buddhist figures
and swirling studs under the slip and glaze; it is of Cizhou type.
Sherds of similar pieces have been excavated at the Yencun kiln in
Huixian, Henan Province from Late Tang/Five Dynasties levels.

41

SMALL YUE JAR WITH OVERLAPPING LOTUS PETALS

PROBABLY NINGBO KILN
ZHEJIANG PROVINCE
LATE TANG TO FIVE DYNASTIES PERIOD
  (9TH OR 10TH CENTURY)
HEIGHT : 14 CM
WIDTH : 7.5 CM

A Yue jar of inverted pear shape with narrow horizontal shoulder and
vertical mouth flanked by small stem-like handles. The body under the
shoulder carved with overlapping lotus petals, all with thin line
striations (other than the bottom row); the pale greyish body is
covered by a pale yellowish, glassy celadon-green glaze of Yue type.
Probably from the Yinxian kiln in Ningbo, Zhejiang Province, though
a Henan kiln is also suggested. Compare Exhibit 74 in the Kiln Sherds
Exhibition, Ashmolean Museum in 1980, for similar leaf treatment.

42

SHALLOW MORTAR WITH COMBED FLORAL PATTERN IN *SANCAI* GLAZES

HUNYUAN KILN, SHANXI PROVINCE
FIVE DYNASTIES PERIOD
  (10TH CENTURY)
DIAMETER : 14.5 CM
DEPTH : 4 CM

A shallow earthenware bowl, the interior of which is combed all over and incised with a stylised five-petalled flower below a combed border and covered with *sancai* glazes. The foot-rim and base are formed by knife parring. Probably from the Hunyuan kiln, Shanxi Province, where comparable sherds have been found. Compare Exhibit 486 in the Kiln Sherds Exhibition, Ashmolean Museum in 1980.

43

WHITE-GLAZED EWER WITH PROTRUDING PETALS

NORTHERN WHITE WARE
FIVE DYNASTIES PERIOD
 (10TH CENTURY)
DIAMETER : 13 CM
HEIGHT : 12 CM

A thinly potted ewer with short circular spout, shallow foot
and globular body, of which the lower half is formed as a large
open flower with protruding petals decorated with incised
stamen-like patterns. The mouth rim is decorated with three
concentric incised lines. The whole piece is covered with a
greenish-white glaze. A similar piece has been excavated from a
tomb at Hefei, Anhui Province which contained a tablet dating
the purchase of the tomb site to 946 A.D. In a recent exhibition at
the National Palace Museum, Taipei, was a bowl with similar
protruding petal decoration, which was described as Ding.

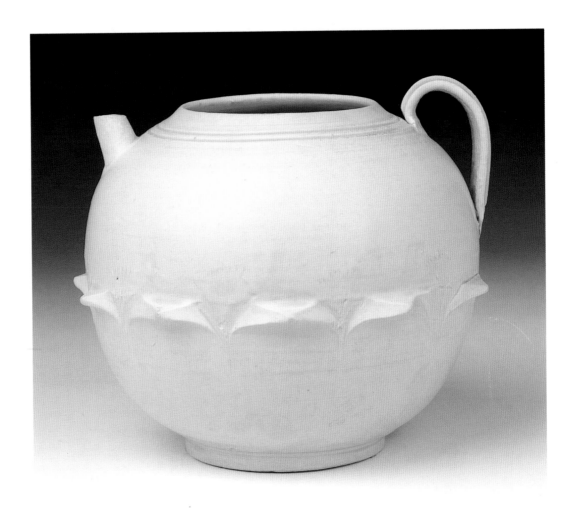

44

CHANGSHA CELADON BOWL OF
FIVE-PETALLED FLOWER METAL
SHAPE WITH BROWN AND GREEN
UNDERGLAZE DECORATION

FIVE DYNASTIES PERIOD
 (10TH CENTURY)
DIAMETER : 14 CM
DEPTH : 5.6 CM

A Changsha bowl of five-petalled flower metal shape, the points
of each petal pinched, the interior decorated with green and brown
stripes radiating from the centre like the stamens of a flower,
all under a crackled green-celadon glaze which extends half way
down the exterior. There is extensive greenish phosphatic pooling in
the centre of the interior and where the glaze on the exterior has
pooled at the edge of the glaze. The bowl has a broad, unglazed
foot-rim of 10th century type.

45

XING COVERED BOX IN
WHITE GLAZE

FIVE DYNASTIES TO EARLY
NORTHERN SONG DYNASTY
  (10TH CENTURY)
DIAMETER : 12 CM
HEIGHT : 7 CM

A thinly potted circular Xing white porcelain covered box with
roughly cut foot-rim, covered all over with a creamy-white glaze.

46

MELON-SHAPED WHITE-GLAZED WINE POT AND COVER

FIVE DYNASTIES TO EARLY
NORTHERN SONG DYNASTY
 (10TH CENTURY)
DIAMETER : 11 CM
HEIGHT : 7.2 CM

A wine pot with cover in the shape of a squat melon with a six-lobed globular body and short, tapering circular spout, a three-ridged strap handle and shallow foot-rim covered with crackled transparent yellowish-white glaze. The base is unglazed revealing a white body with iron impurities and five spur marks. The cover and mouth have four spur marks showing they were fired together, so that any warping would not prevent a fit. This firing method is an early feature. The cover also has a hole for threading a string for tying the cover to the handle. Probably an early white ware from Jingdezhen.

47

YUE CELADON COVERED BOX WITH INCISED SCROLLING FOLIAGE DESIGN

PROBABLY SHANGLINHU KILN
ZHEJIANG PROVINCE
FIVE DYNASTIES TO EARLY
NORTHERN SONG DYNASTY
 (10TH CENTURY)
DIAMETER : 11.3 CM
HEIGHT : 5 CM

A covered Yue box, the top of its cover decorated with incised lotus leaves and feathery fronds. The base has the everted outward sloping foot-rim typical of the period and shows seven silica chip spurs. The box is covered all over with a pale, transparent Yue celadon glaze.

48

WHITE-GLAZED JAR DECORATED WITH CARVED LOTUS PETALS THE COVER WITH LOCKING DEVICE

FIVE DYNASTIES TO EARLY
NORTHERN SONG DYNASTY
  (10TH OR EARLY 11TH CENTURY)
HEIGHT : 28 CM
DIAMETER : 20.5 CM

A bulbous jar and cover, its body carved with overlapping bands of lotus petals extending upwards from the base and from the round mouth down to the shoulder. Three rectangular flanges with cockscomb tops and holes, made to accomodate the round cover, stand at right angles close to the mouth, two on one side and one on the other. The cover has a pointed projection on one side and a vertical flange with a circular hole on the other so that the cover can be locked in place. The whole piece is covered with greenish-white glaze of Ding type. Spur marks round the mouth and cover show that they were fired together. The unusual type of cover and locking device has been found in sherds at Fostat (Egypt) and are known in contemporary Yue ware. It seems probable that a southern provenance is likely, possibly the Chaozhou kilns of northern Guangdong.

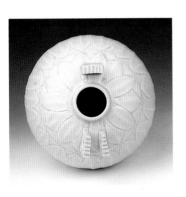

49

A YUE CELADON TRIPLE-JAR COSMETIC BOX WITH LOTUS FINIAL AND BUDS

PROBABLY CHAOZHOU KILN
GUANGDONG PROVINCE
FIVE DYNASTIES TO EARLY
NORTHERN SONG DYNASTY
  (10TH TO 11TH CENTURY)
WIDTH : 7.6 CM
DEPTH : 5.1 CM

A triple-jar cosmetic box, each section of small size and in the form of water chestnuts joined together and surmounted by a lotus flower and pendants buds, the whole covered by a fine, pale celadon glaze of Yue type. Similar boxes, but with *yingqing* glaze, have been found at the Chaozhou kiln in northern Guangdong Province. That kiln also produced Yue-type celadon though no Yue celadon of this design is recorded.

50

CIZHOU PILLOW WITH
INCISED PEONY SCROLLS IN
WHITE AGAINST A REDDISH
RING PUNCH-MARKED GROUND

FIVE DYNASTIES TO EARLY
NORTHERN SONG DYNASTY
 (10TH TO EARLY 11TH CENTURY)
LENGTH : 26.5 CM
WIDTH : 18.2 CM
HEIGHT : 11.7 CM

A Cizhou bean-shaped pillow of Mixian type with incised design
of peony scrolls against a ring punch-marked ground surrounded
by floral scrolls on the top and peony scrolls against a ring punch-
marked ground around the sides. The pillow is covered all over
with a transparent glaze with faintly reddish-brown tint except the
bottom which shows the white-slipped, greyish-brown body. The
air hole is at the top of the back. Note the carry over into the
ceramic medium of the ring punched ground of Tang silver.

51

FIVE-PETALLED CELADON BOWL

PROBABLY YAOZHOU KILN
FIVE DYNASTIES TO EARLY NORTHERN SONG DYNASTY
  (10TH OR EARLY 11TH CENTURY)
DIAMETER : 12.4 CM
DEPTH : 4.4 CM

A Celadon bowl of undecorated five-petalled flower shape, the
interior base flat, the sides sharply angled and lobed, thinly potted,
the base with shallow foot-rim showing a pale greyish body. The
shape is more typical of Xing ware of the 10th century. Experts
have suggested that this is an example of Dong ware. However,
many experts today equate Dong ware with early Yaozhou
celadon, a view with which the author concurs.

52
CELADON BOWL WITH TWELVE PLEATS

PROBABLY YAOZHOU KILN
FIVE DYNASTIES TO EARLY
NORTHERN SONG OR LIAO DYNASTY
 (10TH OR EARLY 11TH CENTURY)
DIAMETER : 12.4 CM
DEPTH : 5.1 CM

Celadon circular bowl of metal shape with twelve exaggerated pleats
from the rim down to the flat interior base. The pale whitish body is
thinly potted and covered with an even, thin, pale yellowish celadon
glaze with extensive bubbles in suspension. The foot-rim slopes from
the flat base, showing oily brown patches under the glaze where it is
thin. A similar piece with less pronounced pleats found in Mongolia
at Baixintun was exhibited in the Cultural Relics of the Northern
Nomads Exhibition held in 1983 in Japan.

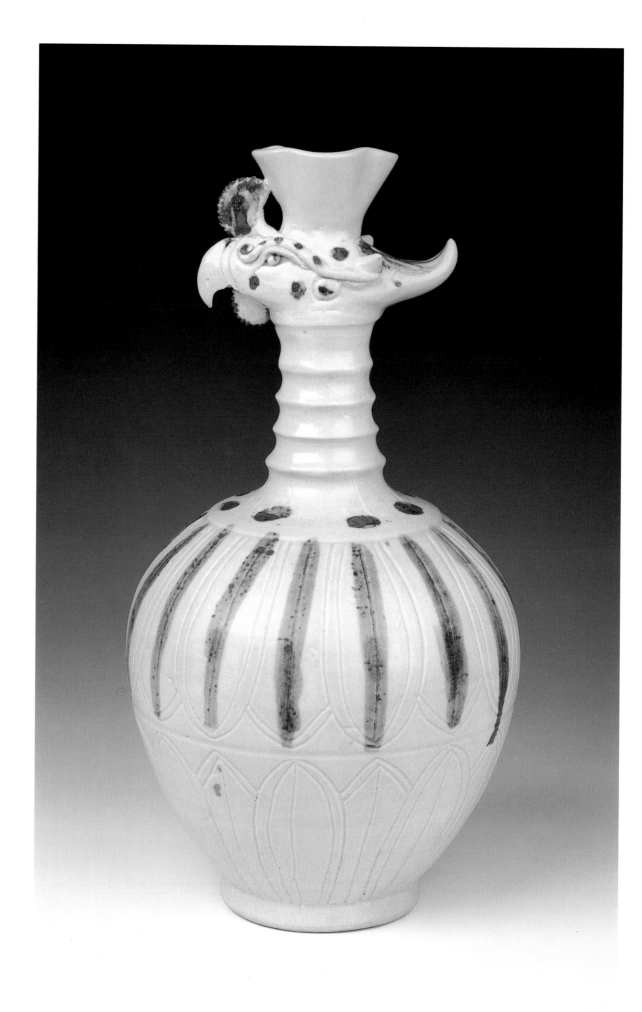

53

PHOENIX-HEADED EWER
WITH BROWN HIGHLIGHTS

SOUTHERN WHITE WARE
FIVE DYNASTIES TO EARLY NORTHERN SONG DYNASTY
  (10TH TO EARLY 11TH CENTURY)
HEIGHT : 33 CM
WIDTH : 17.8 CM

Phoenix-headed ewer, the head sharply sculpted and placed
horizontally at the top of a tall four-ringed slender neck, the head
surmounted by a small petalled mouth, the body decorated with
two bands of overlapping petals down from the shoulder and up
from the base, the whole covered by a shiny white glaze of ivory
tint with numerous ferruginous brown spots on the raised
shoulder and phoenix head and streaks down the centre of the
upper band of petals. Probably from the Chaozhou kiln in
northern Guangdong Province. A similar southern white ware
ewer in the British Museum collection has been exhaustively
discussed.

54

YUE CELADON COVERED BOX WITH PARROT AND FLORAL DESIGNS

EARLY NORTHERN SONG DYNASTY
(LATE 10TH TO EARLY 11TH CENTURY)
DIAMETER : 13.4 CM
HEIGHT : 5 CM

A Yue celadon covered box, its cover decorated with a carved parrot and floral patterns surrounded by a triple band of raised lines and an outer band of impressed scrolls.
The greyish clay body is plain with splayed foot-rim, the base showing traces of a ring of spur marks. The whole box is covered with a greyish celadon glaze.

▶ ## 55

PHOENIX-HEADED BROWN LEAD-GLAZED VASE

LIAO DYNASTY
(LATE 10TH TO EARLY 11TH CENTURY)
HEIGHT : 42.5 CM
WIDTH : 13 CM

A phoenix-headed vase, the phoenix head surmounted by a foliated cup mouth. The phoenix head in the narrow neck only indicated, the tall neck in Tang style with seven ridges, the lower two thirds of the body of graceful jar form slightly pinched in about 2.5 cm from the base. There are two incised lines round the shoulders and three such lines round the pinched section, covered with an orange-brown glaze down three quarters of its length over a white slip. The body of slightly reddish clay.

56
CIZHOU JAR WITH DEEPLY CARVED PEONIES

PROBABLY DENGFENG KILN, HENAN PROVINCE
EARLY NORTHERN SONG DYNASTY
  (LATE 10TH TO EARLY 11TH CENTURY)
DIAMETER : 15 CM
HEIGHT : 14.8 CM

A Cizhou jar of globular shape with slightly everted mouth rim and
flared foot-rim. The grey stoneware body is covered with a white
slip which is deeply carved through the slip to the body with peony
scrolls above a petalled border and below a carved dog-tooth and
petal double-border round the mouth. The whole jar is covered
with a transparent glaze of yellowish-white tone. The base is
unglazed showing the grey body.

57

Bowl with green glaze

Liao dynasty
 (11th century)
Diameter : 11.3 cm
Depth : 6 cm

An earthenware bowl with full body and slightly incurving rim covered both inside and out with a splashed emerald-green glaze over a white slip. The glaze goes down three quarters of the exterior, the unglazed parts reveal the buff body.

58

Shrine with White Glaze

Northern Song dynasty
(11th century)
Height : 11.5 cm
Diameter of plinth : 9.5 cm

A shrine with a figure sitting inside a pavilion surrounded by
a balustrade. The pavilion is reached by an arched bridge which
together with the pavilion stands on a scalloped circular plinth.
The pitched roof is decorated with a fish finial at each end and a
flaming pearl finial in the centre. The piece is covered with a
yellowish-white glaze which also covers the base .

59

EIGHT-PANELLED GLOBULAR
YINGQING EWER WITH HIGH
HANDLE AND COVER

NORTHERN SONG DYNASTY
  (11TH CENTURY)
HEIGHT OF EWER : 17.1 CM
WIDTH : 14.6 CM
HEIGHT OF COVER : 7.6 CM

An undecorated *yingqing* wine ewer of eight slightly concave panels with a double-strap, high looped handle on the shoulder, and a long, faceted spout opposite the handle curving slightly outward. The slightly raised sections of the ewer are accentuated with an incised line on the shoulder and near the base. The hexagonal foot has spur marks. A tall neck of octagonal shape rises between handle and spout; the tall cover of octagonal form is surmounted by a band of eight flanges and topped by a roundel. The cover has two holes for attaching a string; the glaze is of fine bluish colour, the body white and sugary. A *yingqing* ewer of identical shape has been excavated from a Liao tomb at Qianchuanghucun in Chaoyung City, Liaoning Province dated to *circa* 1004. The body of the piece here appears to be from Jingdezhen.

60

A MOULDED DING TYPE BOWL WITH PRECIOUS EMBLEMS, RIBBON-TIED FLORAL SPRAYS, BOYS AND MOTHS

LIAO DYNASTY
(PROBABLY 1ST HALF OF THE 11TH CENTURY)
DIAMETER : 17.8 CM
HEIGHT : 7.0 CM

A moulded bowl with a white glaze of Ding type, the exterior plain with typical Ding teardrops; the interior with a spirally carved flower in the centre, the cavetto with precious emblems such as coral and rhino horn, four small boys with ribbons and moths amid floral sprays of probably peonies and daisies; two of the sprays tied up with ribbons. The glazed rim has a narrow, almost continuous, band of cloud scrolls; the base is unglazed with sand adhering to it; no spur marks; probably from a Ding kiln when under Liao control. The cloud scrolls round the rim and the moths are typical Liao motifs and the glazing of the rims and no spur marks are indicative of the bowl being fired individually in a saggar, in contrast to the later multiple firing of bowls in stepped saggars when the rims remain unglazed.

61

CIZHOU PILLOW WITH BEEHIVE-SHAPED FLORAL DECORATION

NORTHERN SONG DYNASTY
 (11TH CENTURY)
LENGTH : 21.3 CM
WIDTH : 16.7 CM
HEIGHT : 9CM

A Cizhou pillow of oblong four-lobed shape, the top decorated
with a long, beehive-shaped flower against a close, small
ring-punched ground surrounded by a band of incised classic
scroll. The sides decorated with incised stars and circles
alternating in vertical rows in panels, the decoration carved
through the white slip to a brown underslip. The whole
(other than the base) covered by a transparent glassy glaze.

62

CELADON JAR OF ALMS-BOWL
SHAPE AND COVER, THE COVER
WITH TURNED UP EDGE OF
METALLIC INSPIRATION

YAOZHOU KILN
NORTHERN SONG DYNASTY
 (11TH CENTURY)
DIAMETER OF COVER : 13 CM
DIAMETER OF JAR : 12.7 CM
HEIGHT : 7CM

A globular jar of plain alms-bowl shape and cover, the cover of
piecrust form with raised central section and nipple knob, the edge
turned up and over in six places for about 3.2 cm stretches,
covered with a fine glossy celadon glaze of even, slightly greyish
colour, full of bubbles down to about 2.5 cm above the base. The
base shows the typical Yaozhou oily-brown tinge.

63*

CELADON U-SHAPED SHALLOW CIRCULAR
BOWL WITH CARVED PEONIES

YAOZHOU KILN
NORTHERN SONG DYNASTY
  (11TH CENTURY)
DIAMETER : 9.2 CM
DEPTH : 5.4 CM

A Yaozhou celadon U-shaped shallow circular bowl, the exterior
deeply carved with two peony flower heads with leaves on each
side, the interior plain. The celadon glaze of rich greyish-green
colour with extensive pooling and fine bubbles evident throughout.

64

GREEN JUN SAUCER DISH IMITATING *MISE* WARE

NORTHERN SONG DYNASTY
  (11TH CENTURY)
DIAMETER : 21.3 CM
HEIGHT : 3.8 CM

Saucer dish covered overall by an unctious, uncrackled green Jun glaze in imitation of Yue *mise* ware, fired, however, on a square-cut foot-rim in contrast to the spurs or ring of sand used to support Yue *mise* ware.

65

TORTOISE AND SNAKE ON PLINTH WITH WHITE BROWN-SPOTTED GLAZE

NORTHERN SONG DYNASTY
 (11TH CENTURY)
HEIGHT : 11 CM
LENGTH : 8 CM
WIDTH : 7 CM

A tortoise in the coils of a serpent on a rectangular plinth with shaved corners. The head of the tortoise is staring up at the hooded head of the serpent. The whole group is covered with a greenish-white glaze with brown ferruginous splashes. The tortoise and the serpent represent the Sombre Warrior, symbol of the northern quadrant in Chinese mythology.

66

FISH WITH A MAN'S HEAD
ON PLINTH WITH
WHITE BROWN-SPOTTED GLAZE

NORTHERN SONG DYNASTY
  (11TH CENTURY)
LENGTH : 15.5 CM
HEIGHT : 7 CM

A fish with a man's head on a square plinth with shaved corners.
The piece is covered with a greenish-white glaze with extensive
brown ferruginous splashes.

67
STORK AND ROCK WITH WHITE BROWN-SPOTTED GLAZE

NORTHERN SONG DYNASTY
(11TH CENTURY)
HEIGHT : 10 CM

A stork standing on the ground with its body supported by a rock and its short wings outstretched, their tips pointing towards its head. The whole piece is covered with a yellowish-white glaze with extensive ferruginous mottling.

68

Brown-splashed wine/oil pot and cover

Northern Song dynasty
(11th century)
Diameter : 12.7 cm
Height : 9.5 cm

A wine/oil pot and cover, the pot of squat, flattened form with a small mouth 3.2 cm in diameter with a slightly raised rim round the mouth of about 2.5 cm in diameter decorated under the glaze with six large brown ferruginous spots. The spout is very short and rises almost vertically from the edge of the raised section. The small handle has three concave sections and its top is fixed to the body by a flap of clay. The glaze of slightly bluish-white colour, the top of the handle and base of the spout also spotted, the glaze extending most of the way down the exterior to the base; the cover fired separately with a lug for tying a string. It has a spreading plug base and upturned edge. The glaze of the cover is more bluish than on the body.

69

CERAMIC LEATHER BAG-SHAPED BOTTLE WITH GOLDEN-BROWN LEAD GLAZE

LIAO DYNASTY
 (11TH CENTURY)
HEIGHT : 20.3 CM
WIDTH : 11.8 CM

A ceramic, squat, leather bag-shaped bottle, with a short
vertical spout at one corner of the top with a band round the base
of the spout, an arched ceramic glazed handle looped and joined to
the other corner of the top. The bottle is covered almost down to the
base with a rich, dark, golden-brown lead glaze over a white slip, the
unglazed base with shallow foot-rim shows the pinkish white body.

70

DING-TYPE SQUARE SCALLOPED-EDGED
SAUCER DISH WITH MOULDED
DECORATION OF A DUCK WITH WINGS
THREE QUARTERS EXTENDED HOLDING
A FLORAL SPRAY AMID FOLIAGE

LIAO DYNASTY
 (MID 11TH CENTURY)
DIAMETER : 10.6 CM
DEPTH : 3.4 CM

A square saucer dish with flat bottom, and two scalloped-edged sides
angled at 45° from the base. The centre is moulded with a duck
standing with wings three quarters extended, holding a two-flowered
peony spray in its beak. In each of the two top corners there is a
small moth, and the interior base is surrounded by a raised line and
raised dot borders. The outward-sloping sides have moulded peony
sprays and the whole is covered with a white glaze of Ding type but
of somewhat greyish-white tone; the base is unglazed but with sand
adhesions. A sherd of a similar piece is recorded by Wirgin's *Sung
Ceramic Designs* as having been found in a tomb dated 1057 A.D.

71

POLYCHROME CIRCULAR DISH WITH MOULDED FLORAL DECORATION

LIAO DYNASTY
 (LATE 11TH CENTURY)
DIAMETER : 24.8 CM
DEPTH : 5.5 CM

A circular dish with moulded floral decoration of peonies, the interior covered with polychrome decoration of typical green and golden-brown lead glaze splashes on a yellowish-white ground; the outer edge golden brown. There is an inner green-glazed band round an impressed central swirling flower; the exterior is covered with plain golden-brown glaze extending half way to the unglazed foot; there are several spur marks on the green band. The unglazed base with foot-rim shows the slightly pinkish-red body.

72

BLACK AND WHITE MARBLED WARE BOWL WITH WHITE RIM

NORTHERN SONG DYNASTY
  (11TH CENTURY)
DIAMETER : 8.5 CM
DEPT : 4.5 CM

A black and white marbled earthenware bowl with a shallow foot-rim covered inside and out with a transparent glaze. There is a plain white band below the metal-bound rim.

73

PEAR-SHAPED SIMULATED MARBLED WARE VASE WITH TRUMPET MOUTH

CIZHOU WARE
NORTHERN SONG DYNASTY
(11TH CENTURY)
HEIGHT : 22.2 CM
WIDTH : 9.5 CM

A Cizhou pear-shaped vase with trumpet mouth decorated with painted black, brown and white simulated marble glaze on a white slip, the body of buff-coloured clay; the white slip extending almost to the foot-rim.

74

CIZHOU WHITE-RIMMED *TEMMOKU* TEA BOWL

NORTHERN SONG DYNASTY
(11TH CENTURY)
DIAMETER : 12.1 CM
DEPTH : 5.2 CM

A white-rimmed *temmoku* tea bowl with slightly everted rim, the narrow foot and base unglazed showing a close-grained blue-grey body, the interior and exterior with mirror-black glaze, the white-glazed rim slightly overlapping at the join showing extensive crackling and some earth discolouration. The colour of the body indicates its Cizhou origin. Similar contemporaneous bowls were more commonly made in Henan but the body material there has a buff colour.

75

HENAN *TEMMOKU* EARTHENWARE GUAN JAR

NORTHERN SONG DYNASTY
(11TH CENTURY)
WIDTH : 33 CM
HEIGHT : 23.5 CM

A large Henan *temmoku* earthenware Guan jar covered in the
interior and three quarters of exterior with a shiny black *temmoku*
glaze with some brown suffusions. The base has a *bi*-type foot,
reminiscent of late Tang bowls, showing the white clay body.
There are four spur marks in the centre of the interior.

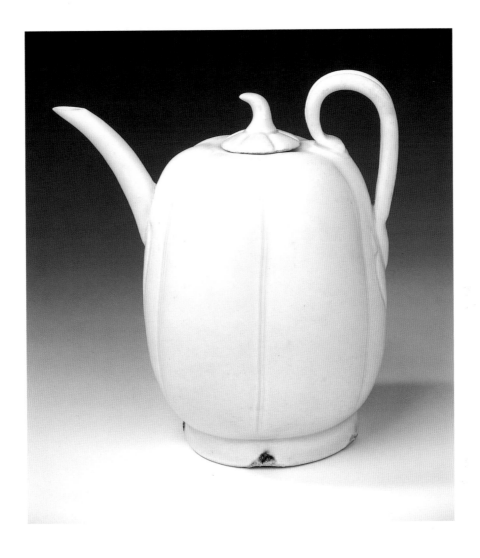

76

YINGQING MELON-SHAPED
EWER WITH STOPPER

NORTHERN SONG DYNASTY
 (*circa*1100 A.D.)
HEIGHT : 14 CM
DIAMETER : 11 CM

Ewer in the shape of a melon with a long outward-curving spout,
the stopper shaped as the end of a melon stalk. The handle is
formed by a double strap. The thinly potted body is covered with a
blue *yingqing* glaze. The base shows several spur marks. A similar
ewer has been excavated from a tomb dated 1099 A.D.

77

Large globular jar decorated with a broad band of carved peonies against an in-filled black ground

Konwa ware
Liao dynasty
  (late 11th to early 12th century)
Width : 31.8 cm
Height : 26.7 cm

A large jar of plain globular shape with thick rolled rim, decorated with a broad band of flowers in white with combed details, the background of the band carved away and in-filled with black glaze with extensive brown suffusions. The rest of the jar has a yellowish-white glaze. The base has a broad *bi*-type foot unglazed without a foot-rim showing the body of putty coloured clay; Konwa ware, sometimes also called Chifeng ware.

78

JUN BRUSHWASHER

LATE NORTHERN SONG DYNASTY
  (LATE 11TH TO EARLY 12TH CENTURY)
DIAMETER : 18.3 CM
DEPTH : 6 CM

A thickly potted Jun brushwasher covered all over with a
lavender-blue glaze. The flat glazed base has three small spur
marks and the Chinese character for 'two'. This piece compares
closely with imperial Jun pieces in the imperial collection, now in
the National Palace Museum in Taipei.

79

LARGE JUN CIRCULAR TRIPOD JAR

NORTHERN SONG DYNASTY
 (LATE 11TH TO EARLY 12TH CENTURY)
DIAMETER : 18 CM
HEIGHT : 13.8 CM

Large, deep Jun circular tripod jar with slightly everted rim
covered by a thick, even lavender-blue glaze. The base is fully
glazed with five spur marks.

80

YINGQING BOWL WITH INCISED CHRYSANTHEMUM DESIGN

LATE NORTHERN SONG DYNASTY
 (EARLY 12TH CENTURY)
DIAMETER : 17.1 CM
DEPTH : 5.8 CM

A *Yingqing* bowl fired on the rim, the base glazed, the interior incised with a chrysanthemum in the centre, the cavetto with four flower heads with incised details and leaves; all under a glaze of bluish tone. Probably Jingdezhen or Nanfeng kiln.

81

YAOZHOU CELADON BOWL WITH CARVED PEONY DESIGN

LATE NORTHERN SONG TO JIN DYNASTY
(LATE 11TH TO EARLY 12TH CENTURY)
DIAMETER : 21.3 CM
DEPTH : 8 CM

A Yaozhou celadon bowl decorated on the interior with a carved design of a single peony and leaves, the details of which are accentuated by comb hatching. The exterior of the bowl is decorated with vertical incised lines. The bowl is covered with a bubbly olive-green celadon glaze.

82

YINGQING BOWL WITH
CARVED PRUNUS SPRAY AND
NEW MOON DESIGN
ITS OUTSIDE GLAZED BLACK

LATE NORTHERN SONG DYNASTY
  (LATE 11TH OR EARLY 12TH CENTURY)
DIAMETER : 13 CM
DEPTH : 4.5 CM

A porcelain bowl with slightly curved sides. The interior is decorated with a carved white prunus spray and crescent moon under a white *yingqing* glaze. The exterior and solid base with no foot-rim are covered with a thick, black crackled glassy glaze. The rim is unglazed.

83

CIZHOU VASE WITH
UNDULATING RIM DECORATED
WITH BLACK PAINTED PEONIES

LATE NORTHERN SONG DYNASTY
  (EARLY 12TH CENTURY)
HEIGHT : 22 CM
DIAMETER : 10 CM

A Cizhou vase with an ovoid body, tall neck, and trumpet-shaped
undulating mouth standing on a hollow everted foot. The buff
stoneware body is covered with a white slip and then painted in
black on either side with a spray of peony with incised details all
under a transparent glaze.

84

SHALLOW CELADON BOWL WITH CARVED FLORAL DECORATION

LATE NORTHERN SONG OR EARLY
SOUTHERN SONG DYNASTY
(12TH CENTURY)
DIAMETER : 15.2 CM
DEPTH : 5.2 CM

A shallow celadon bowl rising from a comparatively small foot. The rim is thin and slightly curved in and the centre of the interior has a button simulating the centre of a flower; the cavetto is carved with a freely drawn lotus flower and three-petalled sagittarius leaves with incised combing under a double-lined border, all under an even blue-green, celadon glaze; the base is unglazed. The style resembles Northern Song Yue ware, but the base and body indicate a slightly later date and a southern provenance. It seems, however, to have been fired on a ring of sand and may be Yue ware or more likely from one of the better celadon producing centres copying Yue wares at the start of the Southern Song dynasty.

85

CIRCULAR CELADON COVERED BOX WITH FLORAL DECORATION IN LOW RELIEF IMITATING CONTEMPORARY KORYU CELADON

EARLY SOUTHERN SONG DYNASTY
  (*circa* 1127 - 1150)
DIAMETER : 11.7 CM
HEIGHT : 4.4 CM

A circular celadon covered box, the cover and base fired together, the sides with muiltiple ridges in low relief, and the cover with similar ridges in the broad outer ring. The central medallion is 7cm in diameter, with floral sprays in low relief probably of camellia and convolvulus flowers all under a blue-green celadon glaze; the protruding base is solid and unglazed without spurs; probably from the Longquan kiln. The colour of this box is the preferred colour of the period and the decoration and colour closely imitate contemporary Koryu celadons, which would, however, have been fired on silica spurs or a ring of sand.

86

EIGHT-BRACKETED YAOZHOU
CELADON SAUCER
DISH WITH MOULDED AND
CARVED FLORAL DECORATION

JIN DYNASTY
 (12TH CENTURY)
DIAMETER : 20 CM
DEPTH : 2.2 CM

An eight-bracketed flat, circular saucer dish with flattened rim of Yaozhou
celadon. The narrow rim is moulded with lotus leaves and flowers and
sagittarius leaves, the interior with a large carved lotus flower, pod, leaf
and sagittarius leaves tied in a bunch; the cavetto is moulded in brackets
corresponding to the rim. The reverse is undecorated, the base without a
foot-rim and unglazed, all under a transparent bubbly celadon glaze of
yellowish celadon colour, pooling in places.

87

CIZHOU OCTAGONAL PILLOW
WITH INCISED DESIGN OF GOOSE
AND LOTUS IN POLYCHROME GLAZES

EARLY JIN DYNASTY
  (12TH CENTURY)
LENGTH : 28 CM
WIDTH : 18.5 CM
HEIGHT : 8.5 CM

A Cizhou octagonal pillow, the body of which is covered all over
with a white under-slip, the top decorated with an incised scene of
a white goose in a green lotus pond within a three-lobed white
diamond-shaped medallion, and four incised yellow peony sprays.
The six sides are incised with peony or lotus sprays. The pillow is
covered with white, yellowish-brown and green lead glazes. The
base is unglazed. The air hole is at the top of the rear side.

88

DING BOWL WITH MOULDED FLORAL AND TWIN-FISH PATTERNS

JIN DYNASTY
  (12TH CENTURY)
DIAMETER : 17 CM
DEPTH : 6 CM

A Ding bowl with shallow unglazed foot-rim and conical body, the interior of which is divided into six panels decorated with lotus, magnolia and prunus sprays. The central medallion shows two fish swimming amid weeds. The exterior is undecorated. The bowl is covered with characteristic ivory-white glaze.

89

DING LIGHT-BROWN,
BEAN-SHAPED PILLOW CARVED IN
SGRAFFITO TECHNIQUE WITH
LOTUS DESIGNS

JIN DYNASTY
(12TH CENTURY)
LENGTH : 30 CM
WIDTH : 21.8 CM
HEIGHT : 17 CM

A large Ding bean-shaped pillow the top of which is decorated in sgraffito technique with a lotus surrounded by classic scrolls with combed hatching through a light-brown iron oxide-derived coating. The sides are decorated with chrysanthemum patterns in the same technique. The pillow is covered with a transparent glaze of creamy tint except for the unglazed bottom. A sherd of a similar pillow has been found at the Ding kiln site. The air holes are on the reverse.

90

BLACK DING EYE-GLASS SHAPED PILLOW WITH CROSS-HATCHED MOULDED SIDES

JIN DYNASTY
 (12TH CENTURY)
WIDTH : 22.9 CM
LENGTH : 23.3 CM
HEIGHT : 12.7 CM

An eye-glass shaped pillow, the pedestal decorated with cross-hatched moulding all under a thick black *temmoku* glaze extending almost to the unglazed base, which shows the putty-coloured Ding body and two air holes. The piece is of very light weight typical of the Ding kiln; the top has numerous small brown flecks and its edge is whitish where the glaze is thin. This black Ding example lacks the white underslip of Cizhou *temmoku* and the coarse-grained heavy body and tendency to brown suffusions at the edges of Henan *temmoku*. Compare with Exhibit 103.

91

DATED *TEMMOKU* GLOBULAR JAR AND COVER

PROBABLY ZIBO KILN, SHANDONG PROVINCE
JIN DYNASTY
  (1168)
HEIGHT : 12.7 CM
WIDTH : 11.4 CM

A globular jar and cover, the rim with a white slip dribbling down the body in ridges which were formed by a knife. It is covered almost to the base and inside with a black *temmoku* glaze tending to a speckled brown-black where there is no underglaze slip. The body is buff where unglazed, and the foot-rim has five spur marks. The cover has a white slip on top and bottom, covered on the top with brownish-black glaze. The handle is shaped like a flower stem. The underside of the cover has a black ink inscription dating it to the 1st month of the 26th year of the Jin emperor Dading (1168) and the character "hung".

92

Yaozhou Persimmon-Red Glazed Tea Bowl of Lotus-Pod Shape

Jin dynasty
(12th century)
Diameter : 10.8 cm
Depth : 4.4 cm

Tea bowl of lotus-pod shape with everted rim glazed all over
(other than the base and foot which reveal the Yaozhou body)
with a completely suffused persimmon-red glaze.

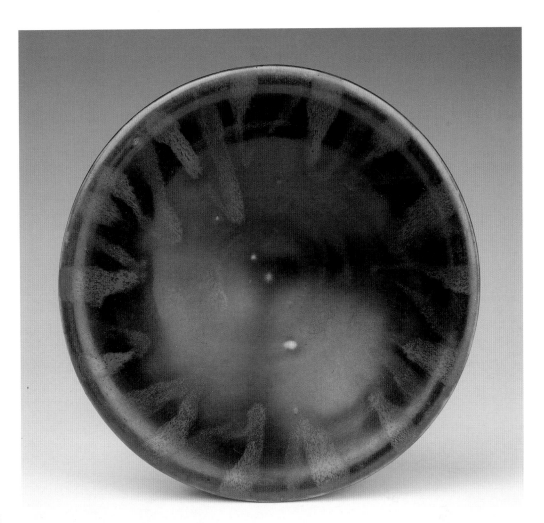

93*

YAOZHOU *TEMMOKU* GLAZED TEA BOWL WITH CURSIVE BROWN CHEVRONS ROUND THE EDGE

JIN DYNASTY
  (12TH CENTURY)
DIAMETER : 14 CM
DEPTH : 4 CM

Shallow tea bowl with slightly everted rim glazed all over (other than the base and foot which reveal the typical Yaozhou foot and body) with an unusual purplish-brown-black *temmoku* glaze of dark aubergine colour, the rim decorated round the edge with cursively drawn brown chevrons.

94

MOULDED DING BOWL WITH LONG RIBBON-TAILED PHOENIXES

JIN DYNASTY
  (LATE 12TH CENTURY)
DIAMETER : 22.6 CM
DEPTH : 6.5 CM

A moulded Ding bowl of classic shape, its small central section decorated with a spiral six-petalled flower, the cavetto with two long, ribbon-tailed phoenixes amid camellia scrolls under a frieze of mono key-fret, fired on its unglazed rim, the exterior undecorated, the base and foot-rim glazed, the creamy-white glaze with minute bubbles and, in places, characteristic teardrops.
An example of this pattern is in the British Museum collection.
This design can be dated fairly closely by dated ceramic moulds of 1184 and 1204 discussed by Wirgin in his book *Sung Ceramic Designs*.

95

DING-TYPE BOWL WITH DEER

JIEXIU KILN, SHANXI PROVINCE
JIN DYNASTY
  (LATE 12TH CENTURY)
DIAMETER : 10.8 CM
DEPTH : 4.1 CM

Ding-type bowl, the white glaze covering finely moulded
decoration in the interior of deer in varying postures in landscapes
within six compartments separated by raised lines. In the centre is
a swirling flower head surrounded by an unglazed band,
characteristic of this kiln, and a glazed band of stylised waves.
The foot-rim is unglazed and the exterior undecorated.

96

LONGQUAN CELADON
VASE OF PEAR SHAPE

SOUTHERN SONG DYNASTY
  (LATE 12TH CENTURY)
HEIGHT : 14 CM
WIDTH : 7.6 CM

A small, plain celadon vase of pear shape with wide-shaped
mouth, the body of grey tone, the thick glaze of even bluish-green
celadon colour.

97

TEMMOKU BOWL OF ALMS-
BOWL SHAPE WITH PARTRIDGE
FEATHER FLECKING

JIAN WARE, FUJIAN PROVINCE
SOUTHERN SONG DYNASTY
  (12TH CENTURY)
DIAMETER : 12.8 CM
DEPTH : 6.5 CM

A bowl of alms-bowl shape with incurving rim, its purplish-brown
body covered both inside and out with a black *temmoku* glaze
suffusing to brown at the edge. The interior, and to a lesser degree
the exterior, has orange-brown flecks radiating from the centre, a
glaze effect sometimes referred to as 'partridge feather' glaze. The
base has a circular indentation and shallow foot, both unglazed,
revealing the typical purplish-brown body of this kiln.

98

JIZHOU BOWL WITH
SKELETON LEAF ON A *TEMMOKU*
GLAZED BACKGROUND

SOUTHERN SONG DYNASTY
  (12TH CENTURY)
DIAMETER : 10.5 CM
DEPTH : 5 CM

A Jizhou tea bowl with slightly everted rim covered inside and out
with a mat brownish-black *temmoku* glaze with a large yellowish-
brown skeleton leaf on the interior.

99

COVERED DING BOWL WITH PERSIMMON-RED GLAZE

JIN DYNASTY
(12TH CENTURY)
DIAMETER : 7.8 CM
DEPTH : 6 CM

A red Ding covered bowl with unglazed foot-rim, showing the whitish-buff, semi-translucent body. The rim is white and the inside is covered with a white crackled glaze. The knob on the cover is in the shape of a peach. The bowl and cover are covered on their exterior with a golden-brown glaze of so-called persimmon-red colour, the base showing in places the black from which, by suffusion, the persimmon-red glaze was derived. Probably from the Yanshan kiln at which kiln site a sherd of a similar piece of Ding ware has been discovered.

100
SAUCER DISH WITH INCISED POMEGRANATE SPRAY IN POLYCHROME GLAZES

JIN DYNASTY
(12TH TO 13TH CENTURY)
DIAMETER : 13 CM
DEPTH : 2.8 CM

An earthenware saucer dish incised with two sprays of pomegranate in yellow with reddish-brown seeds and green leaves and stem. A thin yellow band separates the centre from the flattened rim which is covered with a broad band of green glaze. The exterior and the base are unglazed showing the thin white underslip as well as the buff body. This type of ware was made in Manchuria and is sometimes classified as Liao but most dated examples are of 13th century date.

101
LONGQUAN CELADON MALLET VASE

SOUTHERN SONG DYNASTY
 (LATE 12TH OR EARLY 13TH CENTURY)
HEIGHT : 27 CM
DIAMETER : 10 CM

A Longquan plain mallet vase with long neck and flat everted lip covered with an even celadon glaze of *kinuta* colour, the recessed base is also glazed.

102

LONGQUAN GUAN-TYPE
TEA BOWL WITH CRACKLED
CELADON GLAZE

SOUTHERN SONG DYNASTY
 (LATE 12TH OR EARLY 13TH CENTURY)
DIAMETER : 9 CM
DEPTH : 3.5 CM

A small Guan-type bowl covered with an even bluish-green
celadon glaze with black crackles. The mouth rim and foot-rim are
unglazed, revealing the brownish-black body. Probably from
Longquan.

103

HENAN OCTAGONAL PILLOW
MOULDED WITH CHILD ON
HORSEBACK AND FLORAL
PATTERNS UNDER A BLACK
TEMMOKU GLAZE

JIN DYNASTY
  (12TH TO EARLY 13TH CENTURY)
LENGTH : 23 CM
WIDTH : 18.5 CM
HEIGHT : 13 CM

A Henan octagonal pillow with its front panel moulded with the
scene of a boy riding a winged horse amid foliage. The two
adjacent panels are decorated with lotus while the reverse panel
contains a floral spray. The whole piece is heavy, in complete
contrast to the black Ding pillow (Exhibit 90). It is covered with a
black *temmoku* glaze suffused with brown in places, particularly at
the rim. The base is unglazed and shows the rather coarsely-
grained buff body typical of some Henan *temmoku* ware. The air
hole is at the back, again in contrast to its position on Exhibit 90.

104

SGRAFFITO BOWL WITH FLORAL PATTERN

HUNYUAN KILN, SHANXI PROVINCE
JIN DYNASTY
 (12TH OR EARLY 13TH CENTURY)
DIAMETER : 18.7 CM
DEPTH : 4.5 CM

A shallow circular bowl, the interior with a circular unglazed
section round the centre for kiln staking, a feature characteristic of
many Shanxi kilns. The interior and rim are covered by a white
slip. The interior has two incised rows of petals carved through to
the buff body of the piece in sgraffito style to accentuate the shape
of the flecked and incised petals, the whole (other than the unglazed
ring) covered by a transparent glaze of slightly greyish-green hue,
the low flat foot-rim is also unglazed, Hunyuan kiln, Shanxi
Province. Compare with Exhibit 492 (a sherd of a similar piece
from the Hunyuan kiln) in the Kiln Sherds Exhibition at the
Ashmolean Museum in 1980.

105

JIZHOU VASE WITH PAINTED FLORAL DESIGNS AND INSECTS

SOUTHERN SONG DYNASTY
 (12TH TO 13TH CENTURY)
HEIGHT : 16.5 CM
DIAMETER : 12 CM

A Jizhou stoneware vase of almost *meiping* shape with a flat
everted lip. Decorated directly onto the body with freely drawn
lotus, hibiscus and peony, separated by butterflies in brownish-
black glaze all covered by a transparent glaze. The base is
unglazed revealing the buff body. This piece copies the products of
Cizhou (see Exhibit 83) but is distinguishable by the body material
and the absence of a white slip.

106

YINGQING BOWL WITH
MOULDED PEONY SPRAYS
IN DING STYLE

SOUTHERN SONG DYNASTY
 (12TH TO 13TH CENTURY)
DIAMETER : 14.5 CM
DEPTH : 4 CM

A thinly potted porcelain bowl with small foot-rim and inverted
mouth rim. The interior is decorated with moulded designs of
peony sprays below double-line borders surrounding a single
peony at the centre. The piece is covered by a bluish *yingqing* glaze.
The exterior is undecorated while the mouth rim is unglazed. The
design copies Ding but a southern provenance, probably
Jingdezhen, is certain.

107

CARVED BROWN-GLAZED
SGRAFFITO CIZHOU-TYPE
MEIPING VASE

JIN DYNASTY
 (LATE 12TH OR EARLY 13TH CENTURY)
HEIGHT : 38.1 CM
WIDTH AT SHOULDER : 17.8 CM

A tall Cizhou *meiping* vase of characteristic chicken-leg shape with narrow base and conical mouth; the
body carved in sgraffito technique with three horizontal bands, the top broad, horizontal band with
three large lotus blooms and foliage framed by carved double lines above and below the band. Next a
narrow band of incised classic scroll similarly bordered, the remaining broad band of erect overlapping
lotus petals between double-incised borders. The whole vase is covered with a thick dark-brown glaze
carved through the white slip to the putty-coloured body, which is scraped to form the background.
Cizhou-type pieces were made in many parts of China, principally in the north and northwest. Cizhou
pieces similar to this example were popular products in the then quasi-independent kingdom of
Western Xia, and this example was probably produced in that kingdom during the period indicated.

108

LONGQUAN GUAN-TYPE SHALLOW BOWL WITH CRACKLED CELADON GLAZE

SOUTHERN SONG DYNASTY
 (13TH CENTURY)
DIAMETER : 12.2 CM
DEPTH : 4 CM

A Longquan Guan-type brushwasher with flat base and steep sides covered all over with finely crackled pale bluish-green celadon glaze. The base rim is unglazed revealing the dark body.

109

SMALL STEMMED BULBOUS VASE WITH FLORAL DECORATION

HENGSHAN KILN, HUNAN PROVINCE
SOUTHERN SONG TO JIN DYNASTY
 (13TH CENTURY)
HEIGHT : 13 CM
WIDTH : 11 CM

A small stemmed bulbous vase. The body is of purplish-brown
clay, the neck, lip and interior covered with dark yellowish-green
glaze. The central section is painted with two sprays of lotus in
green and brown on a thin greyish glaze. The stemmed foot and
bottom section are unglazed, but have a purplish-brown slip.

110

TEMMOKU HENAN JAR IN
THE SHAPE OF A TRUNCATED
LOTUS BUD WITH SILVERY
OIL SPOTS

JIN DYNASTY
(13TH CENTURY)
DIAMETER : 11 CM
HEIGHT : 9.2 CM

A small Henan stoneware jar of truncated lotus-bud shape covered
by a black *temmoku* glaze with extensive silvery oil spots. The base
is unglazed showing the greyish body.

111

DATED JIZHOU BOWL WITH BLACKISH-BROWN GLAZE AND YELLOWISH SLIP

SOUTHERN SONG DYNASTY
 (1225 - 1227)
DIAMETER : 16 CM
DEPTH : 7 CM

A Jizhou earthenware bowl with slightly everted rim, the blackish-brown glaze covered inside and out with freely-drawn yellow slip. The lower part of the unglazed exterior is inscribed in black ink on the buff body with Chinese characters which date the bowl to the 19th day of the 8th moon of the period 1225-1227.

112

JIZHOU BOWL WITH PAPER-CUT DESIGN OF TWO PHOENIXES AND SIX-PETALLED FLOWER HEADS IN TORTOISE-SHELL GLAZE

SOUTHERN SONG DYNASTY
 (13TH CENTURY)
DIAMETER : 14.5 CM
DEPTH : 5 CM

A Jizhou conical-shaped tea bowl decorated on the interior with two phoenixes on each side, each facing the centre, and three six-petalled prunus flower heads in paper-cut technique. The bowl is covered with a tortoise-shell glaze. The base is unglazed revealing the greyish-buff body.

113

JIZHOU PEAR-SHAPED VASE
WITH TORTOISE-SHELL GLAZE

SOUTHERN SONG DYNASTY
  (13TH CENTURY)
HEIGHT : 12 CM
WIDTH : 8.6 CM

Jizhou pear-shaped vase with slightly extended vertical section
near the lip with tortoise-shell glaze both inside and out, the unglazed
base with shallow foot-rim showing the greyish-buff body.

114

TEMMOKU-GLAZED CIRCULAR
JIZHOU FLOWER POT WITH
CUT-OUT PRUNUS SPRAYS

SOUTHERN SONG DYNASTY
 (13TH CENTURY)
DIAMETER : 11.7 CM
HEIGHT : 9.8 CM

Temmoku-glazed circular Jizhou flower pot, the base unglazed with
three stubby feet showing the greyish-buff body, the sides almost
vertical, the mouth with horizontally turned-in rim. The sides and
rim covered with brownish black *temmoku* glaze dribbling into the
interior, the sides with two large unglazed silhouettes of prunus
sprays which were covered during the glazing process.

115

JIZHOU *TEMMOKU* GLAZED BOWL WITH GILDED DECORATION OF GOOD LUCK CHARACTERS IN SHAPED MEDALLIONS

SOUTHERN SONG DYNASTY
 (13TH CENTURY)
DIAMETER : 11.3 CM
DEPTH : 5.4 CM

A Jizhou *temmoku* bowl tending to brown where the glaze is thin, the interior painted in gold with four six-petalled flower-shaped medallions surrounding good luck characters, the flowers surrounded by gold lines radiating from the small flat centre, the exterior with a plain black glaze extending two-thirds of the way down. The base is knife-parred and unglazed, revealing the buff body.

116

JIEXIU BOWL WITH MOULDED PEONY SCROLL AND LIONS

JIN DYNASTY
  (13TH CENTURY)
DIAMETER : 18 CM
DEPTH : 4.7 CM

A shallow bowl with greyish-brown body, the interior of which
is decorated with a moulded design of lion-like animals among
spiky foliage bordered above by lozenge patterns and by wave
patterns below. The bowl is covered inside and out with a dark
brownish-green glaze except for the lower portion of the exterior,
the base and a circular band for stacking near the centre of the
interior, which encircles a glazed spiral flower. From Jiexiu
kiln, Shanxi Province.

117

WHITE-RIMMED CELADON BOWL WITH MOULDED PEONY SCROLLS

JIEXIU KILN, SHANXI PROVINCE
JIN DYNASTY
  (13TH CENTURY)
DIAMETER : 18 CM
DEPTH : 7.5 CM

A bowl with greyish-brown body, the interior of which is
decorated with finely moulded peony scrolls. The bowl is
covered inside and out with a dark brownish-green glaze except
for the lower portion of the exterior, the base and a circular
band for stacking at the centre of the interior which encircles a
glazed spiral flower. The edge of the bowl is covered with a
white slip. A sherd of a similar piece from the Jiexiu kiln,
Exhibit 464, was included in the Kiln Sherds Exhibition held at
the Ashmolean Museum in 1980.

118

BLUE-GLAZED JUN TRIPOD
CENSER WITH EXTENSIVE
PURPLE AND RED SPLASHES

JIN DYNASTY
  (13TH CENTURY)
DIAMETER : 5 CM
HEIGHT : 4 CM

A small Jun censer with three small legs covered all over with a
thick bluish glaze with extensive purple and red splashes.

119

CELADON BOWL WITH
CARVED DESIGN OF A PRUNUS
SPRAY UNDER A CRESCENT MOON

LATE SOUTHERN SONG DYNASTY
(13TH CENTURY)
DIAMETER : 11.2 CM
DEPTH : 4.5 CM

A small tea bowl with carved design of a prunus spray and a
crescent moon covered all over with a celadon glaze. This design
was particularly popular in the Southern Song at the Nanfeng
kiln, Jiangxi Province, and this bowl may be from that kiln.

120

TEMMOKU RICE-MEASURE
JAR IMITATING JIZHOU WARE

GANZHOU KILN, JIANGXI PROVINCE
SOUTHERN SONG DYNASTY
 (13TH CENTURY)
WIDTH : 8.9 CM
HEIGHT : 8.3 CM

A small jar of so-called rice-measure shape (probably a tea caddy)
with rolled lip above a vertical section about 2.5 cm deep, the rest
of the jar swelling out and angled in towards the base. The jar is
covered with a brown-black *temmoku* glaze with white phosphatic
splashes, the lower quarter and base are unglazed, showing the
light brown body; the interior is black and brown; the glaze of
Jizhou *temmoku* type. The body material and typical Ganzhou
shape, however, indicate that the nearby Ganzhou kiln is a more
likely provenance for this piece.

121

YINGQING BOWL WITH
CARVED PRUNUS SPRAY
AND NEW MOON DESIGN,
THE RIM AND DESIGN
WITH BROWN SLIP

NANFENG KILN, JIANGXI PROVINCE
LATE SOUTHERN SONG DYNASTY
  (MID 13TH CENTURY)
DIAMETER : 11 CM
DEPTH : 4 CM

A conical bowl with everted brown-slipped rim, the interior of
which is decorated with an incised prunus spray and a new moon
in brown slip. The whole piece is covered with finely crackled
yingqing glaze. The base and the lower part of the exterior are
unglazed. The inner rim is covered with a brown slip. A sherd of an
identical piece from the Nanfeng kiln, Jiangxi Province, dated to
the late Southern Song was included in the Kiln Sherds Exhibition,
held at the Ashmolean Museum in 1980.

122

A *YINGQING* BOWL OF SLIGHTLY
FLARED U-SHAPE, THE CAVETTO
DECORATED WITH PRUNUS SPRAY
CRESCENT MOON AND CONSTELLATION
REFLECTED IN A POND IN THE CENTRE

LATE SOUTHERN SONG DYNASTY
(13TH CENTURY)
DIAMETER : 14.3 CM
DEPTH : 7CM

A *yingqing* bowl of slightly flared U-shape, the cavetto with a
moulded spray of five-petalled prunus, a crescent moon and a
constellation (three stars) reflected in a pond in the centre, the
reverse plain. The piece was fired on the narrow unglazed rim, the
foot is shallow and covered with a glaze of slightly blue tone.
Probably from the Nanfeng kiln or a copy of a Nanfeng kiln
design from Jingdezhen.

123
CIZHOU SEATED LADY WITH POLYCHROME OVERGLAZE ENAMELS

JIN OR EARLY YUAN DYNASTY
 (13TH CENTURY)
HEIGHT : 22.9 CM
WIDTH : 12.4 CM

A graceful lady seated on the edge of a circular stool, on which
one of her sleeve-covered hands rests, the lady looking slightly to
the right, the whole covered by a white slip and decorated with
polychrome overglaze enamels at one of the Cizhou kilns. Her jet-
black hair is parted in the middle with an oval medallion in green
against a bunched-up cloth cap with traces of red. Her upper robe
is green with black floral patterns and black petal zig-zag border.
There is also a loose yellow belt and a long white black-bordered
scarf draped over her shoulder and tied in a bow at the back. The
scarf has floral patterns in green and red enamels. The lower dress
formerly had a red overglaze enamel that has now largely gone,
the stool is glazed black.

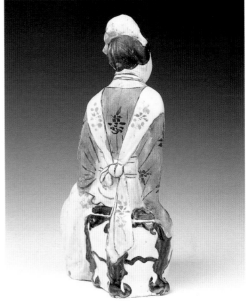

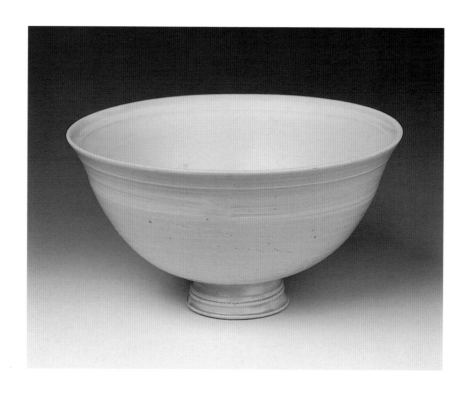

124

A WHITE-GLAZED STEMMED BOWL

HUOXIAN KILN, SHANXI PROVINCE
LATE JIN OR EARLY YUAN DYNASTY
 (13TH CENTURY)
DIAMETER : 11.2 CM
DEPTH : 6 CM

A white-glazed stemmed bowl, the steeply rounded sides with
flared rim and numerous concentric potting lines springing from a
short, hollow, splayed stem. It is covered overall with a transparent
ivory-tinted glaze of Ding type pooling slightly on the interior,
with five small, neat spur marks in the centre, the unglazed base of
the stem revealing the white porcellaneous ware and five additional
spur marks on the rim of the stem.

Compare : Exhibit 465 in the Kiln Sherds Exhibition at the
Ashmolean Museum in 1980. This kiln has been identified as the
Peng kiln of literature, whose products Cao Zhao, an early Yuan
commentator on Chinese ceramics, described as "new Ding ware".

125

CIZHOU VASE WITH
IRON-RUST FLORAL SPRAYS
ON A BROWNISH-BLACK
GROUND

LATE JIN TO EARLY YUAN DYNASTY
 (13TH CENTURY)
HEIGHT : 17.5 CM
DIAMETER : 16 CM

A Cizhou vase with globular body and small mouth with a ridge at
the neck, decorated on the upper half of the body with two iron-
rust floral sprays over the black glaze.

126

RUST-DECORATED *TEMMOKU*
WATERWELL AND WATER
DROPPER IN THE SHAPE
OF A CIRCULAR DRUM
WITH FISHHEAD SPOUT

HENAN KILNS
SOUTHERN SONG OR EARLY YUAN DYNASTY
  (13TH CENTURY)
DIAMETER : 10.2 CM
THE SPOUT : 1.3 CM

A waterwell and water dropper combined in the shape of a circular
drum with a small open-mouthed fish head as the spout. The putty-
coloured Henan body is covered to three quarters of its depth with
a thick black *temmoku* glaze with metallic brown flecks swirling
round the small central hole in the top like a chrysanthemum
flower, with further brown flecking on the sides.

127

GANZHOU STUDDED RICE-MEASURE JAR

GANZHOU KILN, JIANGXI PROVINCE
SOUTHERN SONG TO YUAN DYNASTY
  (13TH TO EARLY 14TH CENTURY)
WIDTH : 11.4 CM
HEIGHT : 8.9 CM

Stoneware jar of so-called rice-measure shape (probably a tea caddy) with rolled lip above a waisted unglazed vertical section about 2.5 cm deep, decorated all round with yellowish-white glazed studs spaced at 1.3 cm intervals. The exterior swelling body is also unglazed with close parallel incisions simulating basket work. The clay is of light chocolate-brown colour, the interior and rolled lip covered by a rust-red iron oxide glaze; a typical Ganzhou kiln jar. Compare with Exhibit 120 in this exhibition. A similar piece was recovered from the Korean Sinan wreck dated *circa* 1323, and is published in the exhibition catalogue of those finds (exhibit 131). Sherds from the Ganzhou kiln were also included in the Kiln Sherds Exhibition held at the Ashmolean Museum in 1980, (see Exhibit 251).

128

JIZHOU BOWL WITH DESIGN
OF AN OPEN STYLISED FLOWER,
THE PETALS WITH DECORATION
SIMULATING *GURI* LACQUER IN
TORTOISE-SHELL GLAZE

YUAN DYNASTY
  (LATE 13TH TO EARLY 14TH CENTURY)
DIAMETER : 12.2 CM
DEPTH : 5 CM

A Jizhou tea bowl covered all over with a blackish-brown
glaze, the interior showing a large, open, stylised five-petalled
flower with *guri*-type scrolls on its petals in yellow slip on the
blackish-brown glaze.

129

LONGQUAN CELADON
TRIPOD CENSER WITH DRAGON
AND ANIMAL MASK APPLIQUES

YUAN DYNASTY
  (LATE 13TH TO EARLY 14TH CENTURY)
DIAMETER : 12.7 CM
HEIGHT : 10.6 CM

A Longquan celadon tripod censer, the globular body of which is
supported on three stubby legs issuing from moulded monster
heads, the sides divided by vertical flanges rising to the short
stepped shoulders beneath the everted rim. The neck is applied
with three dragon appliqués while the body is decorated with three
animal mask appliqués.

130

Cizhou sgraffito pear-shaped vase with carved phoenixes and classic scroll

Early Yuan dynasty
 (late 13th to early 14th century)
Height : 29.5 cm
Diameter : 18 cm

A Cizhou stoneware pear-shaped vase with bulbous body, long neck and everted lip of typical *yuhuchun* shape, decorated in the central horizontal section with two phoenixes among clouds, one with a five-streamer ribboned tail and one with a two-streamer clobbered classic scroll tail. The top section has a stylised lotus petal pattern border and the bottom section a clobbered classic scroll border all done in sgraffito technique, in which the vase is carved through the white slip to the buff body and then covered by a transparent glaze. The foot and base are unglazed, showing the buff body. The depiction of phoenixes with differing tails as here seems a common feature in the Yuan period.

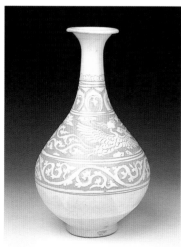

131

YINGQING MEIPING VASE
WITH CARVED PEONIES DESIGN

YUAN DYNASTY
  (LATE 13TH TO EARLY 14TH CENTURY)
HEIGHT : 31 CM
DIAMETER : 18 CM

A *meiping* vase, the body of which is decorated with a broad band
of carved peony scrolls with incised details delineating the leaves,
bordered by overlapping swirling petals on the upper part and tall
lotus petals round the lower half. The vase is covered with a glossy
bluish *yingqing* glaze. The decoration is similar to that found on
Longquan celadon wares of the Yuan dynasty.

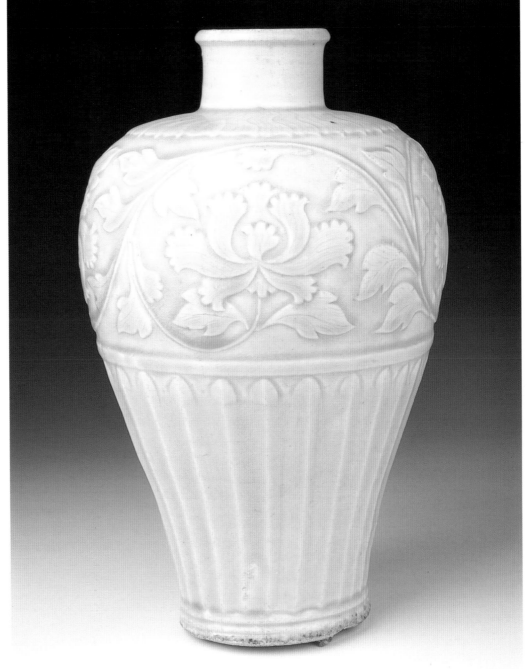

132

MINIATURE GUAN CELADON
DOUBLE-GOURD VASE WITH
ELEPHANT-HEAD APPLIQUES

YUAN DYNASTY
(14TH CENTURY)
HEIGHT : 8.6 CM
WIDTH : 5.8 CM

Miniature double-gourd vase with elephant-head appliqués on
each side of the upper section, the whole covered by a very thick,
broadly crackled, greyish celadon glaze of Guan type, probably
from Longquan. The base is glazed while the shallow foot-rim is
unglazed and of blackish-brown colour.

133

SHUFU SAUCER WITH CARVED
LOTUS IN DING STYLE

YUAN DYNASTY
 (14TH CENTURY)
DIAMETER : 13.5 CM
DEPTH : 3 CM

A *shufu* circular saucer, the interior carved in Ding style with a
single lotus flower and a few leaves all under a bluish *shufu* glaze, the
base unglazed and showing a round, orange iron firing discolouration.
A similar carved *shufu* was recovered from the Sinan wreck off Korea,
which has been dated to *circa* 1323.

134

SMALL *TOBI SEIJI* CELADON KUAN JAR AND COVER

YUAN DYNASTY
 (14TH CENTURY)
DIAMETER : 7.5 CM
HEIGHT : 6.3 CM

A small celadon circular *kuan* jar and cover, the glaze of even celadon colour with extensive ferruginous brown spots in a style called by the Japanese *tobi seiji*, the cover plain with wavy edge.

135

YINGQING BOWL WITH POMEGRANATE DESIGN

YUAN DYNASTY
  (EARLY 14TH CENTURY)
DIAMETER : 11 CM
DEPTH : 4 CM

A six-lobed bowl with steeply rounded sides and metal bound rim, the interior of which is decorated with a moulded central medallion of prunus above water, with a reflection of the crescent moon above, encircled by a band of fruiting pomegranate growing from leafy scrolled stems below a key-fret band. The piece is covered with a *yingqing* glaze of bluish tint. A similar bowl was recovered from the Sinan wreck off Korea which has been dated to *circa* 1323.

136

YINGQING WATER DROPPER,
THE SPOUT EMERGING FROM
A DRAGON'S HEAD, THE HANDLE
FORMING ITS STYLISED BODY

YUAN DYNASTY
 (FIRST HALF OF THE 14TH CENTURY)
DIAMETER : 7 CM
HEIGHT : 6.2 CM

An octagonal water dropper, with ribbed sides and small spout
emerging from a stylised dragon's head. The stylised body of the
dragon forms the handle. The whole is covered with a bluish
yingqing glaze.

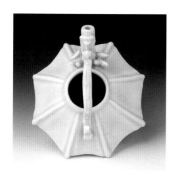

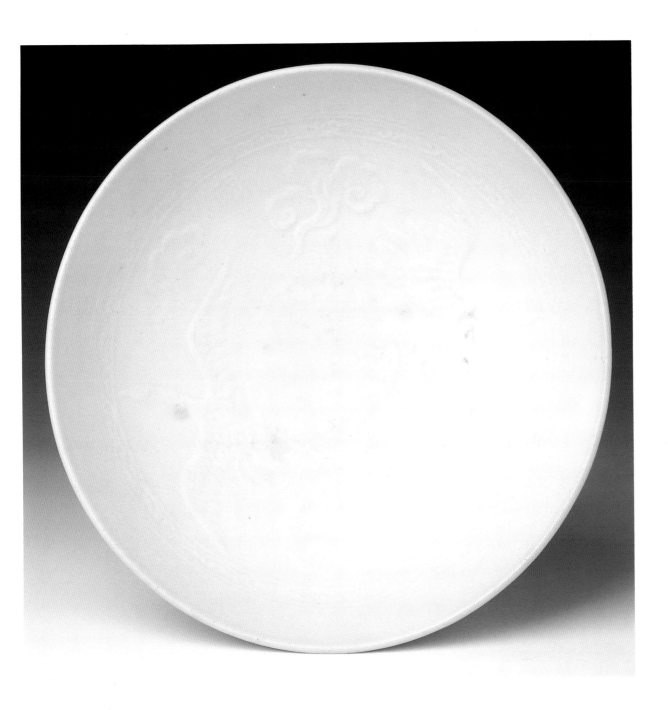

137

SHUFU BOWL WITH
MOULDED CLOUDS,
CHINESE CHARACTERS
FU AND LU
AND GEESE IN FLIGHT

YUAN DYNASTY
 (FIRST HALF OF THE 14TH CENTURY)
DIAMETER : 18.5 CM
DEPTH : 6.3 CM

A shallow bowl with small foot, decorated on the interior with
a moulded design of two wild geese among clouds, bordered by
a band of classic scroll near the rim. The characters *fu* and *lu*
amid the clouds. The exterior is incised at the rim with a wave
pattern and with an incised four-line lotus petal border round
the base. The piece is covered with an opaque *shufu* glaze of
bluish tint.

138

ZHEJIANG CELADON DEEP DISH WITH MOULDED PEONY TREE AND INCISED DECORATION

YUAN DYNASTY
(14TH CENTURY)
DIAMETER : 33 CM
DEPTH : 7.8 CM

A Zhejiang celadon deep dish with an unusual turned-in then everted rim; the centre with a moulded peony tree, and the cavetto with an incised scroll decoration; the exterior with similar incised scroll between incised borders and lotus leaf tips with combed centres. The round base has an unglazed ring; the whole with an even yellowish-green celadon glaze.

139

YINGQING JAR SPLASHED WITH
FERRUGINOUS BROWN SPOTS

YUAN DYNASTY
 (MID 14TH CENTURY)
HEIGHT : 16 CM
DIAMETER : 7.5 CM

A small vase with globular body, long flanged neck and
slightly everted foot covered in *yingqing* glaze and splashed
with underglaze ferruginous brown spots.

140

A BLUE AND WHITE LOBED
GARLIC-HEADED VASE WITH
CHRYSANTHEMUM DECORATION
AND HEXAGONAL STAND.

YUAN DYNASTY
  (MID 14TH CENTURY)
HEIGHT OF VASE : 15.6 CM
WIDTH OF VASE : 7.9 CM
HEIGHT OF STAND : 7.9 CM
WIDTH OF STAND : 7.3 CM

A blue and white lobed garlic-headed vase of pear shape with a
horizontal flange where the neck is narrowest. The main
decoration on the body consists of four chrysanthemum heads
joined by scrolling swept-back leaves between line borders, above
a continuous classic scroll. The neck has lappets below the flange
and spiky leaves above it, the garlic head has pendant petals; the
blue and white stand of hexagonal shape is designed like a six-
legged stool with a round hole in the top to take the vase; the stool
is set on a plinth with a scalloped base, the blue decoration on the
stand is confined to line borders and brackets.

141

BLANC-DE-CHINE JAR
WITH THREE MOULDED
FLOWER SCROLLS AND
FOUR CIRCULAR LUGS

DEHUA KILNS, FUJIAN PROVINCE
YUAN DYNASTY
 (MID 14TH CENTURY)
HEIGHT : 5 CM
DIAMETER : 6.3 CM

A Dehua blanc-de-chine circular jar horizontally luted with
shouldered body and short flared neck, three moulded flowers
scrolling round the shoulder and four small circular lugs set around
the neck, covered with a soft white glaze of ivory tint, the concave
base unglazed. This type of jar continued in production with few
changes of design for several centuries. This example, however,
with its fine moulding was confirmed to be of Yuan date by experts
from Fujian.

142

TRIPOD CELADON CENSER WITH UNGLAZED MOULDED PANELS OF CHILDREN AT PLAY

YUAN TO EARLY MING DYNASTY
(14TH CENTURY)
DIAMETER OF MOUTH : 18 CM
HEIGHT : 10.5 CM

A three-legged censer with a pair of handles in the shape of lions'
heads, the whole covered with a celadon glaze except for two large
rectangular shaped panels on the exterior decorated with moulded
designs of children at play in a garden, reserved unglazed in the
biscuit and fired to an orange-brown colour. The base has a broad,
unglazed disk.

143

DATED CIZHOU *MEIPING* VASE WITH CARVED FLORAL PATTERNS AND INCISED INSCRIPTION IN BLACKISH-BROWN GLAZE

MING DYNASTY
TIANSHUN PERIOD (1464)
HEIGHT : 20.5 CM
DIAMETER : 13 CM

A Cizhou stoneware *meiping* vase, the mouth with tall flanged rim covered with blackish-brown glaze, which is carved through to show the reddish-brown sandy body. The decoration is in three parts, the middle section showing peony scrolls bordered by a band of stylised leaves in the upper part and an incised poem in the lower half in praise of incorrupt officials. Inscribed with the date of the 11th day of the 3rd moon of the 6th year of Tianshun (1458 - 1464), Ming dynasty.

144

SMALL CIRCULAR BLUE AND WHITE DISH DECORATED WITH INTERLOCKING *RUYI* HEADS

MING DYNASTY
CHENGHUA MARK AND PERIOD
 (1467 - 1485)
DIAMETER : 8.3 CM
HEIGHT : 1.9 CM

A small blue and white dish of circular shape, the shallow flared sides at a sharp angle, decorated on the exterior with a frieze of detached stylised lotus sprays divided from a frieze of cloud scrolls beneath the rim by a zig-zag line. The flat centre with a medallion of interlaced *ruyi* heads and lotus buds encloses a circle within a double line border. The underglaze blue of soft tone beneath a waxy texture burnt orange in a thin line where the glaze meets the unglazed foot-rim. The base has a six character underglaze blue mark of Chenghua within a double-line bordered square and the piece is of the period.

145

A BLUE AND WHITE CIRCULAR THREE-LEGGED CENSER

MING DYNASTY
PROBABLY CHENGHUA PERIOD
  (SECOND HALF OF THE 15TH CENTURY)
DIAMETER : 8.6 CM
HEIGHT : 5.4 CM

A blue and white circular three-legged, slightly convex-sided censer, covered, except on the interior, the rim and a patch on the base, with a soft duck-egg white glaze. Decorated with two nicely drawn peony sprays separated by two tadpole-like squiggles with double-line underglaze blue borders at the rim and round the base. A similar censer has been excavated from a Chenghua tomb.

146*

BLUE AND WHITE *MEIPING* VASE
DECORATED IN THE 'WINDSWEPT'
STYLE WITH TWO SCHOLARS
AND ATTENDANTS IN A
LANDSCAPE SETTING

MING DYNASTY
 (SECOND HALF OF THE 15TH CENTURY)
HEIGHT : 31.1 CM
WIDTH : 16.5 CM

Blue and white *meiping* decorated in the so-called 'windswept' style,
the main decoration being of two scholars meeting in a landscape,
their attendants on the reverse, one carrying a *qin*, the other a
dragon-headed staff. The two groups are separated by pine and
willow trees. The reverse with a house entrance and swirling cloud,
the landscape with clouds at the border, two further borders round
the neck, the inner one with four phoenixes amid continuous lotus
scrolls and double-line borders, the outer with false gadroons, the
mouth with four cloud scrolls. A further tall false gadroon border
surrounds the bottom of the vase.

147

SAUCER DISH WITH A WAXY
WHITE GLAZE

MING DYNASTY
ZHENGDE MARK AND PERIOD
 (1506 - 1521)
DIAMETER : 20 CM

A plain saucer dish with shallow foot and slightly everted rim,
covered with a waxy white glaze commonly called 'sweet white'
glaze. The base has a double-ringed four character mark of
Zhengde in underglaze blue. The mark shows the variant in the
upper left character typically found in late Zhengde pieces.

148

IMPERIAL YELLOW
SAUCER DISH

MING DYNASTY
ZHENGDE MARK AND PERIOD
 (1506 - 1521)
DIAMETER : 15.2 CM
DEPTH : 3.4 CM

Imperial yellow saucer dish with even glaze inside and out, of egg-yolk colour, the base with underglaze blue six character Zhengde mark and the piece is of the period.

149

SAUCER DISH WITH
DESIGN OF DRAGONS
IN PURSUIT OF FLAMING
PEARLS WITH CLOUDS IN
GREEN ENAMEL ON A
YELLOW GROUND

MING DYNASTY
ZHENGDE MARK AND PERIOD
 (1506 -1521)
DIAMETER : 20 CM
DEPTH : 4 CM

A porcelain saucer dish with slightly everted rim. The exterior is
decorated with two incised dragons amid clouds in pursuit of
flaming pearls in green enamel on a yellow ground. The base has a
double-ringed four character mark of Zhengde in underglaze blue.
The interior is undecorated.

150

POLYCHROME SAUCER
WITH A SAGE AND
SERVANT IN A LANDSCAPE

MING DYNASTY
ZHENGDE MARK AND PERIOD
  (1506 - 1521)
DIAMETER : 17.1 CM
DEPTH : 3.5 CM

A polychrome saucer decorated in overglaze yellow, light green, aubergine and *rouge-de-fer* enamels with a sage and servant beneath a tree with rocks, grasses and insects in double-ringed medallion surrounded by dots and a cross-hatched diaper border. The reverse has an interrupted lotus scroll in *rouge-de-fer* and green. The base has a six character mark of Xuande in *rouge-de-fer* enclosed in a rectangular frame; the fifth character is written with a stroke variant typically found on late Zhengde pieces.

151

COVERED JAR WITH INCISED
PATTERN OF THE SCROLLING LOTUS
IN AUBERGINE, BROWN AND
YELLOW GLAZES ON A
GREEN GROUND

MING DYNASTY
ZHENGDE TO EARLY JIAJING PERIOD
  (FIRST HALF OF THE 16TH CENTURY)
HEIGHT : 16.5 CM
DIAMETER : 13.5 CM

A covered jar with a globular body and short straight neck, the
emerald-green glazed body of which is incised with lotus scrolls in
yellow, brown and pale aubergine. A *ruyi* band collar is incised on
the shoulder and there are stylised flames round the unglazed base.
The cover is decorated with yellow double circles on a green
ground. The mosque-dome shaped knob is also in yellow.

152

KINRANDE DISH WITH
DESIGN OF PEACH AND
SHOU CHARACTER IN GOLD
ON AN AUBERGINE
GLAZED GROUND

MING DYNASTY
JIAJING PERIOD
 (1522 - 1566)
DIAMETER : 14.5 CM
DEPTH : 1.5 CM

An aubergine *kinrande* four-lobed shallow dish gilded with a
central *shou* longevity character among peach branches within
plain borders. The rim is decorated with gilt bands. The piece is
primarily covered with an aubergine glaze, the base, however,
is glazed yellow.

153

IRON-RED *KINRANDE* BOWL

MING DYNASTY
(MID 16TH CENTURY)
DIAMETER : 12.1 CM
DEPTH : 6.2 CM

A *kinrande* bowl with steeply rounded sides standing on a slightly tapering foot encircling the concave base. Between line borders the exterior is gilded on the rich iron-red ground with a continuous lotus meander with four large blooms among curling leaves. The rim and interior are glazed in white of bluish tint. There is a four character mark, *"Chang ming fu gui"*, "long life, riches and honour", in underglaze blue on the base.

154

COVERED BOX OF FLATTENED
PEACH FORM WITH *CAFE-AU-LAIT*
GLAZE SURMOUNTED BY
AN UNGLAZED PIGEON
HOLDING A SPRAY OF LEAVES

MING DYNASTY
  (SECOND HALF OF THE 16TH CENTURY)
DIAMETER : 8.3 CM
HEIGHT : 7 CM

A covered box of flattened peach form covered with a *cafe-au-lait*
glaze of rather glassy golden tone, the top surmounted by an
unglazed pigeon holding a spray of leaves in its beak.

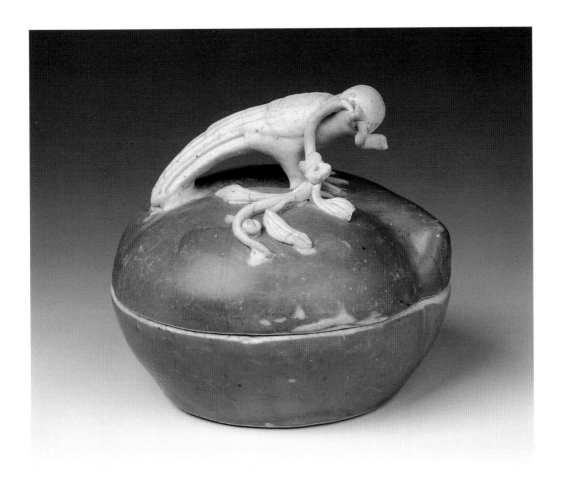

155

WUCAI POLYCHROME SAUCER
DISH DECORATED WITH AN
IMMORTAL AND TWO ATTENDANTS

MING DYNASTY
WANLI MARK AND PERIOD
 (1572 - 1620)
DIAMETER : 15.2 CM
DEPTH : 2.8 CM

A polychrome saucer dish decorated in the *wucai* palette with iron-red, green, yellow and underglaze blue. An immortal stands on a leaf in the centre above breaking waves with an attendant at each side below pine and rockwork, and within a border of auspicious characters amongst scrolling *lingzhi*. The reverse with eight flower sprays above a band of classic scrolls.

156

LOBED BLUE AND WHITE JAR WITH EIGHT DRAGONS CHASING FLAMING PEARLS

MING DYNASTY
WANLI MARK AND PERIOD
 (1572 - 1620)
DIAMETER : 16 CM
HEIGHT : 12.5 CM

An eight-lobed blue and white jar decorated with eight dragons amid clouds in pursuit of flaming pearls set between linked *ruyi* head borders at top and bottom. The band of *ruyi* heads on the shoulder also contains the eight precious emblems.

157

PAIR OF BLUE AND WHITE
PLATES DECORATED WITH
BOYS IN A TUB AND DRAGONS

MING DYNASTY
WANLI MARK AND PERIOD
 (1572 - 1620)
DIAMETER : 17.5 CM
DEPTH : 2.5 CM

Pair of blue and white plates, the centre with three boys in a tub;
one being washed by the other two. There are three boys outside
the tub; one fishing from the terrace balustrade, to one side a palm
tree, the sky with clouds. The cavetto with four five-clawed
dragons chasing a pearl; the reverse with six fruit sprays.

158

SWATOW POLYCHROME DISH
WITH COCKERELS, PAGODA
AND LANDSCAPE DECORATION

LATE MING DYNASTY
 (*circa* 1600)
DIAMETER : 38.1 CM
HEIGHT : 10.9 CM

A Swatow polychrome dish, the centre enamelled with two turquoise
cockerels and flowering plants coloured in brilliant tomato-red and
green. The well with stylised mountains and a pagoda in turquoise
glaze on an island, alternating with sprays of peonies and
chrysanthemums. The lipped rim has a narrow border of tomato-red
circles, and the exterior a single tomato-red line around the rim. There
is much sand adhering to the foot. The white glaze is of characteristic
waxy texture. The use of overglaze turquoise blue in the polychrome
palette seems principally to occur in the kiln producing Swatow wares
and seems to have been confined to the period between *circa* 1550 -
circa 1630. The use of this colour glaze, which tends to chip off easily, at
other Chinese kilns is rare, though contemporary bowls produced
for export to Japan with *kinrande*-associated designs are known and
the colour was occasionally used in early Japanese Arita wares
copying Kraak designs. Swatow polychrome pieces have long been
popular in Japan.

159
SHIWAN *MEIPING* VASE COPYING JUN WARE

LATE MING DYNASTY
 (*circa* 1600)
HEIGHT : 25.3 CM
DIAMETER : 14 CM

A *meiping* vase with slender, ovoid body, short constricted neck
and thick projecting mouth rim, covered with a thick, white,
streaky blue glaze in imitation of Jun ware of the Song dynasty.
The base is covered with a colourless slip revealing the dark brown
body. Probably from Shiwan kiln, Guangdong Province.

160

YIXING JAR COPYING JUN WARE

LATE MING DYNASTY
 (*circa* 1600)
DIAMETER : 30 CM
HEIGHT : 24 CM

A Yixing stoneware jar with globular body, everted mouth and
concave base, covered with a dark blue glaze with milky-blue
suffusions imitating Jun ware. The lower portion and the base are
unglazed, showing the typical reddish-brown body of Yixing ware.

161

KRAAK *CLAPMUTSEN* BOWL
WITH LANDSCAPE, BIRDS
AND FLORAL DESIGNS IN
UNDERGLAZE BLUE

MING DYNASTY
LATE WANLI PERIOD
  (*circa* 1610)
DIAMETER : 22CM
DEPTH : 6.7 CM

A Kraak blue and white *clapmutsen* bowl with everted rim and
foliated border, the centre with a land and seascape showing a
pagoda and boats. The sides of the interior are decorated with four
medallions of herons amid lotus bordered by tassels. The mouth
rim is decorated with scrolling peony. The exterior of the bowl is
also decorated in underglaze blue with four medallions depicting
boys separated by vases. The exterior of the rim shows birds on
floral sprays.

162

BOWL DECORATED WITH
PICNIC SCENE IN
UNDERGLAZE BLUE OF
VARIOUS TONES ON
A *CAFE-AU-LAIT* GROUND

MING DYNASTY
TIANQI PERIOD
  (1621 - 1627)
DIAMETER : 11 CM
DEPTH : 6.5 CM

A bowl decorated with figures, pine, deer and horses in underglaze
blue of various tones on a *cafe-au-lait* ground. The base has a
double-ringed four character mark of Xuande in underglaze blue.

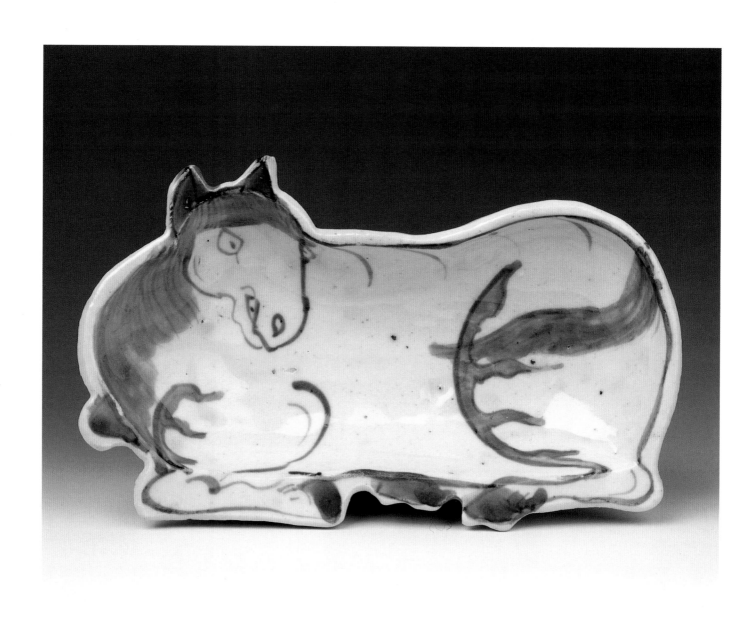

163

A *KO-SOMETSUKE* BLUE AND
WHITE DISH IN THE FORM OF
A RECLINING PONY

MING DYNASTY
TIANQI PERIOD
 (1621 - 1627)
LENGTH : 16.7 CM
WIDTH : 9.3 CM
DEPTH : 3 CM

A blue and white *ko-sometsuke* dish in the form of a reclining pony,
the shallow rounded sides shaped as the body with an
everted rim forming the ears and legs, the features and other
details picked out in underglaze blue. The underside is supported
on four shallow feet and there are areas dappled in blue, with the
pony's head repeated in outline. Dishes in animal form as here
were made in China for the Japanese market, frequently in sets of
five, chiefly in the period from 1620-1645.

164

TWO INCENSE STICK HOLDERS
IN THE FORM OF IMMORTALS
WITH 'EGG AND SPINACH'
GLAZE WITH RED HIGHLIGHTS

LATE MING DYNASTY
  (1600 - 1644)
HEIGHT : 15.6 CM
WIDTH : 6 CM

Ceramic sculptures of Zhong Liquan and He Xianggu, two of the eight immortals, on top of a high pedestal with three circular holes. Zhong Liquan has a high-domed bald head and a long pointed white beard. He is seated with left knee raised on which rests his hand holding his attribute, a fan. His garment is tied with a belt and has long pendulant sleeves. He Xianggu holds her attribute, a ladle. The biscuit is buff-white, the figures and the top of the pedestal covered with pale green, aubergine, yellow and uncoloured glaze of glassy consistency in the palette commonly called 'egg and spinach'. Behind the figures are circular spill holders for incense sticks. Typical Ming dynasty overglaze tomato-red is present on the ladle and fan. These figures can be compared with ivory sculptures of the same subjects from the late 16th/early 17th century. The clay, the high-holed pedestal and the use of overglaze tomato-red fixes their date to the late Ming.

165

BLANC-DE-CHINE CENSER
WITH STRING PATTERN IN
WHITE GLAZE

DEHUA KILN, FUJIAN PROVINCE
LATE MING DYNASTY
 (1600 - 1640)
HEIGHT : 6.5 CM
DIAMETER : 14 CM

A *blanc-de-chine* three-legged straight-sided circular censer, the
body of which is decorated with eight, ridged concave bands. The
whole piece is covered with a transparent creamy-white glaze
except for the base and central part of the interior, which are
unglazed.

166

SLENDER *BLANC-DE-CHINE*
VASE WITH LION-HEAD BOSSES

DEHUA KILN, FUJIAN PROVINCE
LATE MING DYNASTY
 (1600 -1644)
 HEIGHT : 27.9 CM
WIDTH : 10.5 CM

A slender *blanc-de-chine* vase with bubbly pinky-cream glaze with
small Chinese lion-head bosses. A similar vase was found in the
tomb of the Wanli emperor who died in 1620.

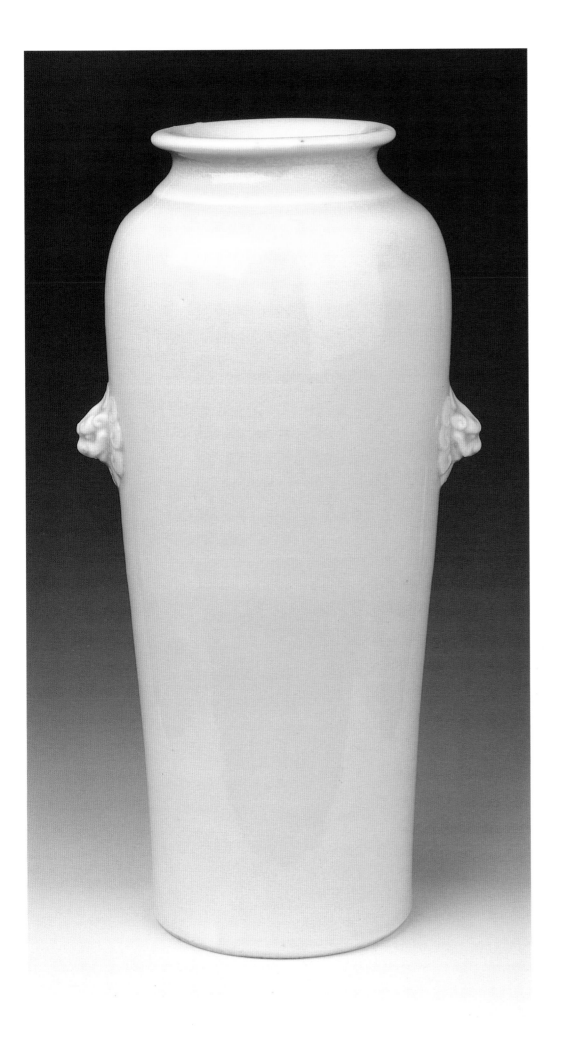

167

A RUST-RED DEHUA CENSER
OF CIRCULAR BULGING
FORM WITH LION-HEAD MASK
ON EITHER SIDE

DEHUA KILN, FUJIAN PROVINCE
LATE MING DYNASTY
 (*circa* 1600 - 1644)
WIDTH : 8.3 CM
HEIGHT : 5.2 CM

A red Dehua censer of circular form with two small lion-head
masks one on each side, the lip sharply everted, the sides bulging
but contracting to the foot-rim, the base revealing the icing sugar-
like body. The whole outside and one third of the interior is
covered with rust coloured brown glaze caused by complete
suffusion of rich iron oxide. This kiln was more famous for its
blanc-de-chine wares, but rust-red as here and purple glazed wares
following *blanc-de-chine* shapes are known.

168

A BLUE AND WHITE INCENSE BURNER DECORATED WITH FLOWERS, WILLOW, GRASSES AND *ANHUA* BORDERS

TRANSITIONAL PERIOD
  (*circa* 1640.)
WIDTH : 9.8 CM
HEIGHT : 7 CM

A blue and white incense burner of circular, slightly bulging form in the lower half, the rim curving out slightly, a border band (1.6 cm wide) of scrolling flowers between line borders in *anhua* technique typical of the period under the rim, a plain incised *anhua* band round the base. The main panel decorated by two groups one of daisies and 'v-tick' grasses drawn up from the base *anhua* border, the other panel of two sprays of prunus and willow fronds going down from the upper *anhua* border, all under a duck-egg white glaze; the base glazed.

169

BOWL WITH MOULDED
DESIGN OF DRAGONS AND
A CARP AMONG WAVES
UNDER A WHITE GLAZE

SHUNZHI TO EARLY KANGXI PERIOD
 (1650 - 1670)
DIAMETER : 11.2 CM
DEPTH : 5.5 CM

A bowl with everted rim, the edge covered by a light-brown slip,
the interior decorated with two moulded dragons in pursuit of a
flaming pearl above waves. The central medallion is decorated
with a carp rising from waves. The whole bowl is covered with a
greenish-white glaze.

170

BLUE AND WHITE VASE DECORATED WITH BAMBOO PINE, PRUNUS AND MAGPIES

EARLY KANGXI PERIOD
 (1662 - 1677)
HEIGHT : 24 CM
DIAMETER : 11 CM

A blue and white vase with a slightly tapering body, slightly everted mouth and flaring foot. The main section is decorated with magpies amid pines, bamboo and prunus sprays with an inscribed poem bordered above and below with a band of wet-drawn splashes typical of the period. The neck is decorated with rocks and chrysanthemums. The base has a six character horizontal Chenghua mark in underglaze blue in two lines of three characters each; the writing of the mark horizontally as here is quite common during this period.

171

BLUE AND WHITE
DISH WITH LANDSCAPE
DESIGN IN
'MASTER OF THE ROCKS' STYLE

EARLY KANGXI PERIOD
  (1662 - 1677)
DIAMETER : 21.4 CM
DEPTH : 4.2 CM

A saucer dish, the interior of which is painted in underglaze blue
with a landscape scene in the 'Master of the Rocks' style. The border
of the dish is decorated with a band of pine needles and groups of
wet-drawn splashes typical of the period. The exterior has three
sprays in underglaze blue. The base has a double-ringed six
character, two line vertical mark of Chenghua in underglaze blue.

172

BLUE AND WHITE TULIP-SHAPED BEAKER DECORATED WITH MAGPIES AND GRASSES

EARLY KANGXI PERIOD
 (1662 - 1677)
HEIGHT : 9.8 CM
WIDTH : 9.8 CM

A tulip-shaped beaker very delicately painted in underglaze blue of pale tone; the exterior is decorated with four magpies, two in flight, two on branches that protrude from bamboo or tree fronds which emphasize the rim; the ground has delicate grasses and wild flowers with *Taihu* rocks; the interior with pencil-drawn, flame-type decoration; the rim is unglazed, as is the base. In its centre is a glazed patch with the six character mark of Chenghua in two vertical lines of three in a single ringed circle.

173

COVERED BOX WITH DESIGN OF LYCHEES AND LOTUS IN UNDERGLAZE BLUE AND RED

EARLY KANGXI PERIOD
 (1662 -1677)
DIAMETER : 13 CM
HEIGHT : 7 CM

A covered box with shallow foot-rim, the cover of which is decorated within a double-ringed circle with lotus sprays surrounded by pomegranates and lychees. The body is decorated with bamboo, rose and chrysanthemum sprays. All branches and leaves are in underglaze blue while the flowers and fruit are in underglaze red. The base has a double-ringed vertical six character mark of Chenghua in underglaze blue, written in bold style typical of the period. The use of wet-drawn splashes in the decoration is also typical of the period.

174

COVERED JAR WITH SCENE OF A BANQUET IN *WUCAI* ENAMELS

EARLY KANGXI PERIOD
 (1662 - 1677)
HEIGHT : 37 CM
DIAMETER : 24 CM

A covered jar with globular body decorated with a design of a garden scene with ladies dancing, bordered above by a band of wet-drawn splashes typical of the period and a wide band of chrysanthemum and peony sprays separated by rocks, all in *wucai* enamels. The cover shows children at play bordered by rocks and trees. The base is unglazed.

175

DATED DISH WITH
LANDSCAPE SCENE IN
UNDERGLAZE BLUE AND RED IN
'MASTER OF THE ROCKS' STYLE

EARLY KANGXI PERIOD
(1671)
DIAMETER : 11.3 CM
DEPTH : 1.5 CM

A small circular dish with slightly everted rim painted on the
interior with a landscape scene with a hermit walking on a bridge
within circular double-line bordered medallion. The hermit, distant
mountains, bridges and trees are all painted in underglaze blue in
the style of the 'Master of the Rocks', except for the foliage of a
tree in the centre, which is drawn in underglaze red. The inner
mouth rim is decorated by a narrow band of classic scroll. The
base is inscribed horizontally "produced by Zhonghetang in the
year of *xinhai* (1671) in the Kangxi period", the foot-rim has a
narrow concave groove forming a double foot-rim, which is
commonly found in this period.

176

A SMALL BOWL WITH STEEP
ROUNDED SIDES WITH
SOUFFLE-BLUE GLAZE

17TH CENTURY
DIAMETER : 8.9 CM
DEPTH : 5 CM

A small bowl with steep rounded sides covered on the exterior
with an unusual rich, dark soufflé-blue glaze, the interior and base
covered with bluish-white glaze.

177

CENSER IN IMPERIAL YELLOW GLAZE

TRANSITIONAL OR KANGXI PERIOD
 (SECOND HALF OF THE 17TH CENTURY)
DIAMETER : 12.2 CM
HEIGHT : 7.2 CM

A cylindrical censer with a band of string pattern in the middle of
the exterior, covered all over with imperial yellow glaze.

178

BLUE AND WHITE AND
UNDERGLAZE RED GINGER
JAR WITH BIRDS, PRUNUS
AND MAGNOLIA WITH
ANHUA HIGHLIGHTS

EARLY KANGXI PERIOD
 (1662 - 1677)
HEIGHT : 19.7 CM
WIDTH : 19 CM

Blue and white and underglaze red ginger jar decorated with birds in flight and on the branch of a cherry tree. There is also a rock with a pheasant near a magnolia tree in full bloom and peonies. Narrow borders of convolvulus, prunus spray, peony and chrysanthemum frame the top and bottom, some details accentuated by incised outlines and *anhua* decoration. The base has the horizontal Jiajing mark in two lines of three in a double circle; but the piece is early Kangxi. The use of incised outlines and *anhua* is rare. The use of *anhua* for formal borders was popular in the preceding Transitional period (see for example Exhibit 168) but here the *anhua* is being used to create only part of the border design.

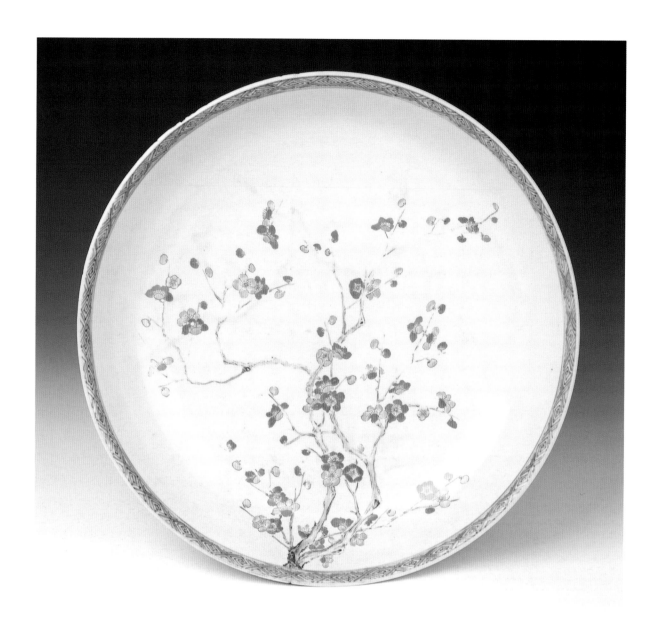

179

LARGE SHALLOW BOWL
WITH PRUNUS TREE IN
ROUGE-DE-FER, AUBERGINE
AND GILDED OVERGLAZE
ENAMELS CONTINUING ON
TO THE REVERSE

KANGXI MARK AND PERIOD
  (1662 - 1722)
DIAMETER : 33 CM
DEPTH : 6.4 CM

Large shallow bowl, the interior edged with *doucai* hatched diaper
decoration, the centre with prunus tree in *rouge-de-fer* and aubergine
overglaze enamels enriched by gilding, the tree trunk continuing
on to the reverse. This latter decorative convention was common in the
succeeding Yongzheng reign but unusual in Kangxi. The base has a six
character mark of Kangxi boldly written in a double-line bordered circle,
The foot-rim has a concave channel forming a double foot-rim a feature
commonly found on early Kangxi pieces. Compare Exhibit 175.
However, the palette and decorative convention noted suggest a mid or
late Kangxi dating as more appropriate.

180

FIVE *SANCAI* BISCUIT
CRUET DISHES OF POINTED
SHIELD SHAPE DECORATED
WITH BUTTERFLIES, INSECTS,
BIRDS AND FLOWERS
OF THE SEASON

KANGXI PERIOD
  (1662 - 1722)
LENGTH : 12.7 CM
WIDTH : 11.1 CM

Each with flat rim with formal flower borders in green and
aubergine on a yellow ground and the reverse with flower sprays in
black on a yellow ground; the dishes are individually decorated as
follows :

(i) Rock, magnolia spray and birds

(ii) Peony sprays, cricket and mosquitoes in yellow, green
    and aubergine

(iii) and (iv) Butterflies and flowers

(v) Three birds in a bare tree

181

CELADON AND UNDERGLAZE
RED BRUSHPOT WITH FLORAL
AND INSECT DECORATION

KANGXI PERIOD
 (1662 - 1722)
HEIGHT : 13.3 CM
DIAMETER : 11.4 CM

A celadon and underglaze red brushpot of circular section,
the exterior with two rectangular panels one carved with a *Taihu*
rock, chysanthemum and insects, the other similarly decorated but
with peonies and an insect; the flowers in each panel in underglaze
red the remainder in light celadon glaze; the interior and base
glazed in white.

182

LANGYAO VASE WITH
LONG NECK

KANGXI PERIOD
 (1662 - 1722)
HEIGHT : 24 CM
DIAMETER : 14 CM

A vase with long neck flaring at the top, covered with a dark
copper-red *langyao* glaze with areas of dark crushed strawberry
mottling, stopping short at the foot. The mouth rim, the interior
and the base are covered in white glaze.

183

WUCAI DISH WITH DRAGONS
AND PHOENIXES AMID FLORAL
DECORATION

KANGXI PERIOD
  (1662 - 1722)
PROBABLY (1662 - 1700)
DIAMETER : 24.8 CM
DEPTH : 3.5 CM

A *wucai* dish of saucer shape with lipped rim, decorated in
wucai enamels including underglaze blue with scaly dragons and
flying phoenixes among chrysanthemum and peony blooms and
dense foliate scrolls, arranged in a medallion within a frieze
repeated on the underside; six character mark of Xuande, but is
first half of Kangxi, .

184

FAMILLE VERTE STEM CUP
OF OCTAGONAL SHAPE
WITH BIRDS AND FLOWERS
OF THE SEASONS

MID KANGXI PERIOD
 (1683 - 1700)
HEIGHT OVERALL : 12.2 CM
DIAMETER : 7.3 CM
HEIGHT THE FOOT : 5.1 CM

A *famille verte* stem cup of octagonal shape, ridged and splayed at base,
with green enamel ring and underglaze blue borders also outlining
the eight panels. It is decorated in an overglaze *famille verte* palette with
(i) magnolia and blue birds (ii) chrysanthemum and butterfly
(iii) narcissus and blue birds (iv) gold flowers and butterfly (v) green
prunus and birds (vi) peony and butterfly (vii) prunus and birds
(viii) ducks, lotus and butterfly. The use here of both underglaze blue
and overglaze blue seems to mark this as an early example of *famille verte*
in which palette normally only overglaze blue appears.

185

FAMILLE VERTE FLAT-
BOTTOMED BOWL IMITATING
LIMOGES ENAMEL

MIDDLE OR LATE KANGXI PERIOD
  (1722)
DIAMETER : 8.2 CM
DEPTH : 4.1 CM

A *famille verte* flat-bottomed bowl with straight outsplayed sides;
the base decorated with a floral spray with black border, the
exterior with five groups of C-scrolls all different, the interior
plain except in the central medallion which depicts fruits and
leaves in a tub and the initials "I.L." all surrounded by a black
border. The enamels are *famille verte* in tone in imitation of a
Limoges enamel piece, the initials being probably those of the
Limoges enameller Jacques Laudin (1627 - 1695) or his nephew
of the same name (1663 - 1729), who both signed their pieces as
shown. It is known that samples of Limoges enamels were given to
Chinese potters by the Jesuits during Kangxi's reign, as mention
is made of this in the Jesuit Father De Mailly's letter of 1720 and
this appears to be one of the items produced from such samples.

186

CHINESE IMARI
ROULEAU VASE

MID KANGXI PERIOD
  (1690 - 1705)
HEIGHT : 41.5 CM
DIAMETER : 15.9 CM

A rouleau-shaped vase of traditional shape decorated in underglaze blue and overglaze green, *rouge-de-
fer* and yellow enamels with gilding, all in imitation of the finest Imari ware of the 1690s, some of the
designs also echoing Japanese Imari. The main decoration consists of four oblong panels with indents
at the four corners depicting (i) a peony by a rock with two birds in flight (ii) two gentlemen and a boy
picnicking under a willow by a stream with a boat, a lady looking on (iii) peonies and a rock drawn in
Japanese Imari style with one bird, and (iv) an archer on horseback shooting deer in a landscape. Each
panel is separated by a brocade ball with pendants and a bell hanging from a canopy, the shoulders
with twelve panels topped by *ruyi* heads, the panels with flowers of the seasons and brocade borders,
the neck with *rouge-de-fer* florettes and bands topped by four floral sprays; other floral sprays and
Buddhist emblems round the bottom of the vase.

187

A SET OF FOUR SMALL
GRADUATED CUPS WITH
FLOWERS, BUTTERFLIES AND
BIRDS IN UNDERGLAZE BLUE
ON A CORAL-RED GROUND

LATE KANGXI MARK AND PERIOD
  (1700 - 1722)
DIAMETER : 4 - 5.4 CM
DEPTH : 2.2 - 3.2 CM

A set of four small cups of different sizes made to fit together
one inside the other, decorated on the exterior with narcissus,
chrysanthemum, butterflies, pines, birds, prunus and rocks in
underglaze blue; the remainder glazed with coral-red enamel.
There is a double-ringed six character mark of Kangxi in
underglaze blue on the base of each cup.

188

A POLYCHROME *YUZHI*
CORAL-GROUND BOWL WITH
FLORAL DECORATION;
FOUR CHARACTER KANGXI *YUZHI*
MARK IN UNDERGLAZE BLUE
WITHIN A DOUBLE-LINED SQUARE
AND OF THE PERIOD

LATE KANGXI MARK AND PERIOD
(1700-1722)
WIDTH : 10.8 CM
DEPTH : 5.4 CM

A coral-ground bowl with slightly flaring rim decorated on the
exterior in a *famille verte* palette with peonies and other varieties of
flowering plants on a dark iron-red ground, the interior plain.
Such *yuzhi* bowls were apparently made to imperial order in the
late Kangxi and Yongzheng periods with those enamelled in the
imperial palace having an overglaze pink enamel four character
mark, and those enamelled elsewhere having an underglaze or
overglaze blue four character mark.

189
CHICKEN CUP IN
DOUCAI ENAMELS

LATE KANGXI PERIOD
  (1700 - 1722)
DIAMETER : 8.2 CM
DEPTH : 3.5 CM

A chicken cup decorated in Chenghua *doucai* style. The base has a
six character underglaze blue mark of Chenghua in a rectangular
cartouche with double-line borders.

190

BOWL WITH *ANHUA* DESIGN OF TWO DRAGONS IN PURSUIT OF A FLAMING PEARL UNDER A WHITE GLAZE

LATE KANGXI MARK AND PERIOD
 (1700 - 1722)
DIAMETER : 18 CM
DEPTH : 5.7 CM

A bowl with *anhua* decoration of two dragons in pursuit of a flaming pearl covered with white glaze.

191

DEEP PURPLE GLAZED BOWL

LATE KANGXI MARK AND PERIOD
(1700 - 1722)
DIAMETER : 12.4 CM
DEPTH : 5.8 CM

Bowl with steep rounded sides, covered both inside and out with a
brilliant dark purple translucent glaze, the glaze deepening in tone
around the base and foot, the foot-rim with three spur marks.

192
PEACH-BLOOM BRUSHWASHER

LATE KANGXI MARK AND PERIOD
 (1700 - 1722)
DIAMETER : 11.4 CM
DEPTH : 3.7 CM

A peach-bloom brushwasher, the steeply rounded sides with a peach-bloom glaze of light mushroom colour, the interior, rim and base glazed in white.

193

A Chenghua-style blue and white palace bowl decorated with camellia and peony

Late Kangxi mark and period
 (1700 - 1722)
Diameter : 15 cm
Depth : 6.4 cm

A Chenghua style palace bowl decorated in underglaze blue on the outside with a continuous scroll of four five-pointed, star-shaped camellia flowers in pairs separated by buds above an overlapping petal border, the interior with continuous peony scroll and a peony in the central medallion.

194

CONICAL BLUE AND WHITE BOWL WITH DESIGN OF *KUI* DRAGON MEDALLIONS

YONGZHENG MARK AND PERIOD
 (1723 - 1735)
DIAMETER : 20 CM
DEPTH : 6 CM

A conical bowl decorated in underglaze blue on the exterior with
kui dragon medallions bordered by stylised double-bird patterns
and stylised waves round the foot-rim. The central medallion in the
interior is also decorated with a *kui* dragon.

195

A LARGE BLUE AND WHITE FISH BOWL IN MING STYLE

YONGZHENG MARK AND PERIOD
(1723 - 1735)
DIAMETER : 39.4 CM
DEPTH : 23.5 CM

A large blue and white fish bowl in Ming style with a wide mouth, the rounded sides tapering to a raised band around the base. It is painted with stylised petal lappets radiating from the shallow ring-foot, below a broad frieze of six meticulously drawn fruiting and flowering branches including peaches, pomegranates, lotus and peony, each rising from a *lingzhi* sprig. The narrow shoulders with trefoil lappets pendant from a collar of wave scrolls at the base of the plain moulded lip, the underglaze blue of vivid tone with extensive heaping and piling to simulate the 15th century prototype; the base with seal mark of Yongzheng.

196

BOWL WITH DESIGN OF NINE DRAGONS IN UNDERGLAZE RED

YONGZHENG MARK AND PERIOD
 (1723 - 1735)
DIAMETER : 13 CM
DEPTH : 6.4 CM

A white porcelain bowl decorated in underglaze copper-red with nine dragons among clouds and above waves, the six character underglaze blue mark in a double-line bordered rectangle.

197

STEM BOWL WITH SPRAYS
OF CITRUS, POMEGRANATE
AND PEACH IN UNDERGLAZE
RED AND BLUE

YONGZHENG MARK AND PERIOD
(1723 - 1735)
DIAMETER : 16.5 CM
HEIGHT : 11.3 CM

A stem bowl decorated with sprays of peach, pomegranate and
citrus, the so-called three abundances. The fruits are drawn in
underglaze red, the leaves and stem in underglaze blue. The
slightly splayed foot is hollow and the white glaze is of bluish tint.
The interior is undecorated. There is a six character mark of
Yongzheng in underglaze blue on the inner wall of the foot. Here
the red glaze appears to be of *langyao* type rather than the more
usual underglaze copper-red.

198

MINIATURE *DOUCAI MEIPING*
WITH FLORAL DECORATION
WITH INSECTS

YONGZHENG MARK AND PERIOD
 (1723 - 1735)
HEIGHT : 9.8 CM
WIDTH : 6.2 CM

Miniature *doucai meiping* decorated with a pomegranate tree and
chrysanthemums issuing from a rock and three bees.

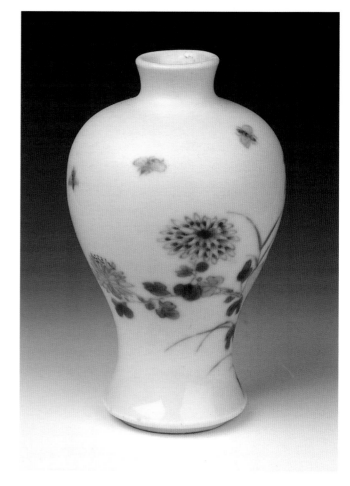

199

DOUCAI BOWL WITH FLORAL
DECORATION

YONGZHENG MARK AND PERIOD
 (1723 - 1735)
DIAMETER : 13.3 CM
DEPTH : 6.5 CM

Doucai bowl, the exterior delicately painted with an elaborate
flower scroll, outlined in underglaze blue and coloured in a widely
ranging palette including a rich purple colour, the interior with a
small medallion in the centre.

200

FAMILLE VERTE PLATE WITH A
SCHOLAR IN A LANDSCAPE WITH
BROAD ORANGE BORDER

YONGZHENG MARK AND PERIOD
(1723 - 1735)
DIAMETER : 20 CM
DEPTH : 4 CM

A plate with rounded sides, the centre decorated in *famille verte*
enamels in Chinese taste with a scholar resting with a *qin* beside a
stream, pine tree and a rock. The cavetto has an orange glaze, the
reverse is plain. The base has a six character horizontal underglaze
blue mark of Yongzheng in double-line circle and is of the period.
Note the use here of overglaze white enamel for the water. The use
of white overglaze enamel was an innovation of *circa* 1720. Before
then the white porcelain on which the overglaze enamels were
placed was used for the white portions of the design.

201

SHALLOW BOWL WITH BROWN GLAZE

YONGZHENG MARK AND PERIOD
 (1723 - 1735)
DIAMETER : 17.5 CM
DEPTH : 5 CM

A shallow bowl with everted rim covered with a *cafe-au-lait* glaze,
the rounded sides encircled by a narrow grooved band.

202

Sacrificial blue-backed saucer

Yongzheng mark and period
(1723 -1735)
Diameter : 15.2 cm
Depth : 3.5 cm

Sacrificial blue-backed saucer with slightly everted rim, the inner surface uncoloured.

203

PALE AUBERGINE GLAZED SAUCER DISH

YONGZHENG MARK AND PERIOD
 (1723 - 1735)
DIAMETER : 11.4 CM
DEPTH : 2.8 CM

A pale aubergine glazed saucer dish, the shallow flared sides engraved on the underside with a continuous band of pomegranates growing from scrolled stems with many curled leaves, the base in white with the underglaze blue mark. Chinese records show that dishes of this colour and design were supplied to the Qing imperial palace in 1729.

204

PAIR OF EMERALD-GREEN GLAZED SAUCER DISHES

YONGZHENG MARK AND PERIOD
 (1723 - 1735)
DIAMETER : 11.4 CM
DEPTH : 2.8 CM

Pair of emerald-green glazed saucer dishes, the reverse incised
under the glaze with the eight precious emblems, the base glazed
white with underglaze blue mark.

205

IMPERIAL
YELLOW SAUCER DISH

YONGZHENG MARK AND PERIOD
(1723 - 1735)
DIAMETER : 14 CM
DEPTH : 3.2 CM

An imperial yellow saucer dish of pale hue, the base with six character
mark of Yongzheng in underglaze blue on characteristic duck-egg
white ground in a double circle.

206

DRUM-SHAPED TRIPOD BULB BOWL WITH ROBIN'S EGG GLAZE

YONGZHENG MARK AND PERIOD
 (1723 - 35)
DIAMETER : 17.5 CM
DEPTH : 5 CM

A three-legged brushwasher in the shape of a shallow drum-shaped bulb bowl. The whole piece is covered inside and out with a robin's egg glaze of somewhat reddish-blue tone. The base has an incised four character seal mark of Yongzheng. This piece shows that at this date the colour glaze fusion necessary for true robin's egg glaze had not been perfected.

207

PAIR OF BOWLS EACH
DECORATED WITH FLORAL
PATTERNS IN *GRISAILLE*
ENAMELS

YONGZHENG MARK AND PERIOD
  (1723 - 1735)
DIAMETER : 9 CM
DEPTH : 4.1 CM

A pair of small bowls of slightly different sizes decorated with
interlocking floral scrolls in blackish *grisaille* enamels. There is a
double-ringed six character mark of Yongzheng in underglaze blue
on the base of each bowl.

208

SMALL CUP INCISED WITH
LOTUS SCROLL IN GREEN
ENAMELS ON AN
IMPERIAL YELLOW GROUND

YONGZHENG MARK AND PERIOD
 (1723 -1735)
DIAMETER : 4.7 CM
DEPTH : 2.5 CM

A small cup decorated on the exterior with incised continuous
lotus scrolls in green enamel on a bright imperial yellow ground.
The base has a double-ringed, six character mark of Yongzheng in
underglaze blue.

209

FAMILLE ROSE SAUCER WITH
FLORAL SPRAYS

YONGZHENG PERIOD
 (1723 - 1735)
DIAMETER : 13.3 CM
HEIGHT : 1.6 CM

A *famille rose* saucer decorated in Chinese taste with a spray of dog
roses and pinks, the reverse with two similar sprays; the base has
the incised inventory mark of the Duke of Saxony's collection, the
inventory of which was drawn up in 1729.

210

BRUSH POT WITH DESIGNS OF BIRDS AND FLOWERS OF THE SEASONS IN *FAMILLE ROSE* ENAMELS

YONGZHENG PERIOD
 (1723-1735)
HEIGHT : 14.7 CM
DIAMETER : 11.7 CM

A square brush pot with pared corners showing simulated woodgrain panels, all edged in simulated brown-speckled, yellowish-green bamboo. The four sides are painted in *famille rose* enamels with four-season designs of birds on floral sprays. The rather muddy rose colour and its sparse use confirms this as an early *famille rose* piece. The use of simulated woodgrain is known as an innovation of the Yongzheng period.

211
DATED VASE WITH LANDSCAPE SCENE IN CELADON AND UNDERGLAZE BLUE AND RED

YONGZHENG PERIOD
 (1731)
HEIGHT : 42 CM
DIAMETER OF MOUTH : 13.5 CM

A vase decorated in underglaze blue and red with mountain landscape designs with rocks in relief covered by a celadon wash. On the trumpet neck is a dedicatory inscription in underglaze blue which includes the date of the 9th year of Yongzheng (1731).

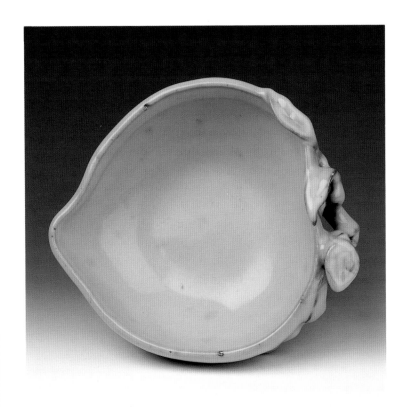

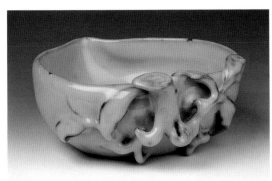

212
GUAN-TYPE GLAZED PEACH SHAPED WATER CONTAINER

YONGZHENG PERIOD
 (1722 - 1735)
WIDTH : 13.3 CM
DEPTH : 5 CM

A water container in the shape of a half peach with some small leaves, covered with a very thick guan-type glaze, the base showing six tiny spur marks.

213

Tea-Dust
Glazed Water Pot

Chenghua seal mark
 (first half of the 18th century)
Diameter : 7.9 cm
Height : 5.1 cm

A tea-dust glazed water pot with large mouth, the sides gently incurving, the glaze turning to brown at the rim and base. The pot
was fired on six small spurs, and the base shows a stamped
four character seal mark of Chenghua.

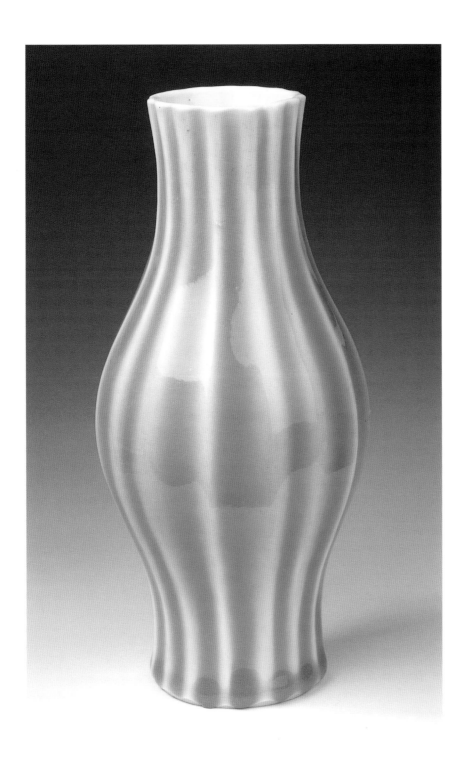

214

RIBBED CELADON-GLAZED VASE

FIRST HALF OF THE 18TH CENTURY
HEIGHT : 19.3 CM
WIDTH : 9.5 CM

A ribbed celadon-glazed vase of tapered form, the steeply rounded sides sloping to a short neck above and tapering to a high-waisted foot below. The foot and neck are very slightly splayed and the sides have sixteen ribs. The glaze pooling darker in the recessed areas and thinning over the ridges; the thickly potted foot and flat, recessed base are unglazed, the interior and lip glazed in white. Similar vases mounted in French ormolu datable to the first half of the 18th century are known.

215

ARMORIAL SOUP PLATE
WITH THE ARMS OF LAMBTON

SECOND QUARTER OF THE 18TH CENTURY
DIAMETER : 22 CM
HEIGHT : 4.8 CM

An armorial soup plate with broad everted rim decorated in its
centre with the arms of Lambton as borne by the Earls of
Durham, consisting of three rams on a black ground with a white
horizontal central bar within a shield. The rim is decorated with
eight floral groups in red, brown, green, turquoise and blue
overglaze enamels with gilding; the cavetto with pendant tassels.

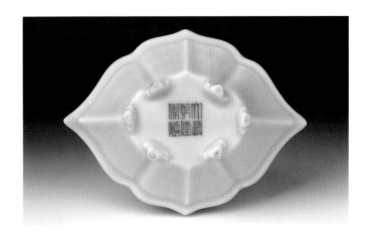

216

FOLIATED DISH WITH PALE CELADON GLAZE

QIANLONG MARK AND PERIOD
 (1736 - 1795)
LENGTH : 12.5 CM
WIDTH : 8.7 CM
DEPTH : 3 CM

A foliated porcelain dish with six small bracket legs covered with
a thick opaque glaze of pale celadon colour.

217

A *CLAIR-DE-LUNE*
BRUSHWASHER

QIANLONG MARK AND PERIOD
 (1736 - 1795)
DIAMETER : 11.4 CM
HEIGHT : 4.1CM

A *clair-de-lune* brushwasher, the baggy sides rising to a lipped rim, the foot-rim covered with a brown slip, the glaze of even, pale blue *clair-de-lune* colour.

218

A GREEN AND YELLOW DRAGON DISH

QIANLONG MARK AND PERIOD
 (1736 - 1795)
DIAMETER : 18.4 CM
DEPTH : 4.1 CM

A green and yellow dragon dish in Ming style (compare
Exhibit 149), the exterior of the shallow sides engraved with two
dragons pursuing flaming pearls amid clouds picked out in green
on a bright imperial yellow ground. The interior, lip and base all
in white glaze, the base with six character seal mark of Qianlong
in underglaze blue.

219

A Ru-type flared dish

Qianlong mark and period
(1736 - 1795)
Diameter : 16.8 cm
Depth : 3.5 cm

A Ru-type flared dish, the narrow sides springing from a foot-rim
of wedge-shaped cross section with a black slip on the edge,
covered overall with a grey-blue glaze of even colour; seal mark of
Qianlong in underglaze blue. It will be noted that the Qing idea of
Ru ware produced at Jingdezhen bears little resemblence to the
Ru wares of the Northern Song, now positively identified from the
discovery in 1986 of the Ru kiln at Qingliangsi village, Baofeng
County, Henan Province.

220

A JARDINIERE OF SQUARED FORM WITH GLAZE IMITATING PUDDING STONE

QIANLONG MARK AND PERIOD
 (1736 - 1795)
POST 1770
DIAMETER : 18.5 CM
HEIGHT : 8.8 CM

A jardiniere of squared form, the body of lozenge shape with wide flared mouth, the whole standing on angular *ruyi* shaped legs, the interior with four holes pierced at the corners, enamelled overall to imitate pudding stone in tones of brown; six character seal mark of Qianlong in gold enamel in a pale brown square panel on the base. This piece is likely to date to the second half of this reign, when ceramics copying other media were increasingly made.

221

Robin's egg vase with green variant glaze

Qianlong mark and period
 (1736 - 1795)
Height : 24.4 cm
Width : 14.5 cm

A robin's egg vase of circular shape with simulated handle projections of *meiping* shape, the whole covered with a rich glaze of predominently green colour with blue overtones (no red). The base is impressed with a six character seal mark of Qianlong.

222

YIXING PEACH-SHAPED BRUSHWASHER

MID QING DYNASTY
(18TH CENTURY)
WIDTH : 7 CM
DEPTH : 2 CM

A Yixing water container in the shape of a half peach with its seed
inside, a small peach to one side and leaves underneath.

223

SEAL BOX AND COVER WITH
LANDSCAPE IN *FAMILLE ROSE*
ENAMELS IN MEDALLIONS
RESERVED ON AN
EMBROIDERED GROUND

LATE QIANLONG MARK AND PERIOD
(1775 - 1795)
LENGTH : 6 CM
WIDTH : 6 CM
HEIGHT : 2.5 CM

A small foliated covered seal box with shallow foot-rim decorated
on the top of the cover with a landscape scene of a pavilion beside
a lake under a rocky cliff within a foliated border, in *famille-rose*
enamels of blue, rose, black and yellow. The other parts of the box
are decorated with stylised floral patterns. The interior and base,
other than the four character seal mark of Qianlong in underglaze
blue, are covered with a greenish-turquoise overglaze as
commonly found late in the reign.

224

SAUCER WITH GREEN DRAGONS ON AN IMPERIAL YELLOW GROUND

JIAQING MARK AND PERIOD
 (1796 - 1820)
DIAMETER : 13 CM
DEPTH : 2.8 CM

Imperial yellow saucer with a jagged edge decorated in
the centre with an imperial (frontally-facing) dragon in green, the
cavetto with two green imperial dragons chasing flaming pearls,
the central dragon surrounded by double black lines with
flowers in green; the reverse with eight floral sprays in green
on imperial yellow ground.

225

YIXING YANG PENGNIAN
STONE WEIGHT SHAPED TEAPOT
WITH OVERHEAD HANDLE IN
PURPLE CLAY WITH CALLIGRAPHY
BY CHEN MANSHENG

QING DYNASTY
 (*circa* 1820)
WIDTH : 13.5 CM
HEIGHT : 13 CM

A Yixing purple clay teapot in the shape of a stone weight with
overhead handle. Both sides of the body are inscribed with poems
by Chen Mansheng otherwise known as Chen Hongshou
(1768 - 1822), a well-known scholar official of the time and a great
patron of Yixing pottery. The calligraphy seems likely to be that of
Chen Mansheng himself. The base bears the seal mark of "The
studio of A Man Tou" in a square cartouche, the studio name of
Chen Mansheng, while the lid is stamped with the seal mark of
Yang Pengnian (fl. 1796-1820), the most celebrated Yixing potter
of the time. It is known that Yang and Chen co-operated to
produce a number of excellent teapots in the early 19th century
which are much treasured and sought after by collectors.